DEATH SHIPS

THE STORY OF LIFE AND DEATH
ON SIX BIG EMIGRANT SHIPS

DOUG LIMBRICK

Other Nonfiction Books by the Author:

From the Wars of the Roses to Colonial Victoria

The *Stag* Diary – Passage to Colonial Adelaide 1850

Farewell to Old England Forever

Running the Marathon with Cancer

For more details see: www.douglimbrick.com

Comments/enquiries to: info@douglimbrick.com

Death Ships Copyright © 2021 by Doug Limbrick

All rights reserved. No part of this book may be reproduced in any form or by any electronic or mechanical means including information storage and retrieval systems, without permission in writing from the author. The only exception is by a reviewer, who may quote short excerpts in a review.

This is a work of nonfiction. The events and conversations in this book have been set down to the best of the author's ability, although some names and details may have been changed to protect the privacy of individuals. Every effort has been made to trace or contact all copyright holders. The publishers will be pleased to make good any omissions or rectify any mistakes brought to their attention at the earliest opportunity.

Printed in Australia

First Printing: July 2021

SHAWLINE
PUBLISHING
GROUP

Shawline Publishing Group Pty Ltd
www.shawlinepublishing.com.au

Paperback ISBN- 9781922594006
Ebook ISBN- 9781922594013

Acknowledgements

A number of people provided invaluable assistance during the course of my writing this book. I am particularly grateful for the resources that are available through the vast collection of material at the National Library of Australia (NLA). Original documents and old manuscripts were readily available through the various library–reading rooms. My thanks go to the staff of the NLA for their assistance and patience. The Woden Valley Branch of the Canberra Library has also been of considerable assistance in locating many publications for me to borrow while researching this project. I would also like to acknowledge the assistance provided by the State Library of South Australia in locating some key documents for me and the assistance provided by the State Libraries of Victoria, New South Wales and Western Australia with pictorial and other material. I also need to acknowledge the assistance provided by the Merseyside Maritime museum, Liverpool, England, and by the New Brunswick Museum, Saint John, Canada. My editor, Dr Pam Faulks, made valuable suggestions during the final drafting process for which I am grateful. A considerable amount of design and graphics assistance has been provided by Jeremy Limbrick, which has considerably enhanced this publication.

Author's Note for readers:

Measures of distance and weight and type of currency have been maintained, as they were in nineteenth-century Britain and the Australian colonies. Hence metric and decimal terms are not used. Thus, to assist readers who may want to convert terms used in this book, the following may be of use:

- 1 mile is approximately equivalent to 1.6 kilometres
- 1 yard is approximately equivalent to 0.9 metres
- 1 foot is approximately equivalent to 0.3 metres
- 1 ton is approximately equivalent to 1.02 tonnes
- 1 ounce is approximately equivalent to 28.4 grams
- 1 gallon is approximately equivalent to 4.5 litres
- 70° Fahrenheit is approximately equivalent to 21° Celsius.

Currency used in this book comprises pounds (£), shillings (s) and pence (d).

This book contains many quotations from historic sources, including letters, diaries, pamphlets and newspapers. In using these quotations,

I have left any misspellings intact and avoided the use of commonly used terms to identify misspellings (such as the Latin word: *sic*). However, there were a small number of quotes that required the insertion of punctuation for the sake of clarity.

This book is dedicated to the 4782 emigrants who set sail for the Australian colonies in six large North American–built ships in 1852, hoping for a new start and a better life.

Fly, brother, fly! More high, more high!
Or we shall be belated:
For slow and slow that ship will go,
When the Mariner's trance is abated.

I woke and we were sailing on
As in a gentle weather:
'Twas night, calm night, the Moon was high;
The dead men stood together.

All stood together on the deck,
For a charnel-dungeon fitter:
All fixed on me their stony eyes,
That in the Moon did glitter.

The pang, the curse, with which they died,
Has never passed away:
I could not draw my eyes from theirs,
Nor turn them up to pray.

The Rime of the Ancient Mariner
Samuel Taylor Coleridge (1798)

Contents

Other Nonfiction Books by the Author: iii
Acknowledgements v
Author's Note for readers: vii
List of Illustrations xvii
Introduction xxi
Chapter 1 - Emigrating to the Colonies 1
Chapter 2 - Emigration and Diseases of Victorian Britain 23
Chapter 3 - Emigrating from Liverpool 37
Chapter 4 - La Trobe, the Gold Rush and the Demand for Labour 51
Chapter 5 - The *Bourneuf* 69
Chapter 6 - The *Wanata* 77
Chapter 7 - The *Marco Polo* 89
Chapter 8 - The *Ticonderoga* 107
Chapter 9 - The *Beejapore* 125
Chapter 10 - The *Shackamaxon* 157
Chapter 11 - Conclusion 177
Appendix A 199
Bibliography 203
Index 207

List of Illustrations

Chapter 1 – Emigrating to the Colonies

1. Diagram of Sail Rigging Comparing a Ship and a Barque.
2. Emigrants at Dinner. Typical scene of steerage-class emigrants beneath the main deck.
3. Sketches on Board an Emigrant Ship 1875.
4. Map Showing the Two Routes to the Colonies.
5. The *Constance* on her passage from Plymouth to Adelaide 1849 by T G Dutton.
6. Sailing in a Big Seas – on Board the *Loch Broom*.
7. Ship *Red Jacket* among Icebergs.
8. The *Stag* in a storm – watercolour by Alexander Weynton.
9. Bright Future 1852 created by George Stafford.

Chapter 2 – Emigration and Diseases of Victorian Britain

10. The Cow Pock or the Wonderful Effects of the New Inoculation, cartoon by satirist James Gillray.

Chapter 3 – Emigrating from Liverpool

11. Canada Timber Docks, Liverpool, Towards the Close of Day by Robert Dudley.
12. George's Dock, Liverpool.
13. The Embarkation, Waterloo Docks, Liverpool.

14. Birkenhead Depot Ground Floor – Communal Eating.

15. Quarter Deck of an Emigrant Ship – the Roll Call.

Chapter 4 – La Trobe and the Gold Rush and the Demand for Labour

16. Bright Visions or the Gold Diggings created by George Stafford.

17. Gold Washing Fitz Roy Ophir Diggings 1851 by George Francis Angas.

18. Disembarking and Off to the Diggings 1852.

19. Alarming Prospect: Single Ladies off to the Diggings 1853 by John Leech.

20. Charles Joseph La Trobe by John Botterill.

21. Canvass Town in 1853 by S.T. Gill.

22. Puddling 1852 by S.T.Gill.

Chapter 5 – The *Bourneuf*

23. The *Bourneuf* Docked at Birkenhead 1852.

24. Below Decks Sketch of Ship *Bournef*.

25. Yarra Street Pier Geelong by T.W. Cameron.

Chapter 6 – The *Wanata*

26. A Typical New Brunswick Ship Yard.

27. New Brunswick Harbour.

28. Passengers Arriving in Melbourne After Quarantine.

Chapter 7 – The Marco Polo

29. James Smith ca. 1851 (with ***Marco Polo*** in the background).

30. Carvings on Stern of ***Marco Polo***.

    . Head of *Marco Polo*.

    . *Marco Polo* Reclining (Eastern Dress).

31. ***Marco Polo*** by John Goodchild.

32. *Marco Polo* 1859 by Thomas Robertson.

33. *Marco Polo* by J Johnson.

34. Captain Arnold ca. 1870.

35. Inscribed Silver Tea Service

36. *Marco Polo* by D M Little.

Chapter 8 – The *Ticonderoga*

37. Williamsburg Waterfront & Harbour 1850.

38. Map of Port Phillip.

39. Quarantine Ground Port Phillip Bay ca. 1851 by Thomas Ham.

40. Hobson's Bay & Williamstown, Port Phillip ca. 1850.

41. Queens Wharf, Melbourne 1850s by S.T. Gill.

Chapter 9 – The *Beejapore*

42. Typical Ship Construction (***Revolving Light*** - 1338 tons) New Brunswick.

43. Market Slip, St. John, New Brunswick.

44. Sketch of Ship ***Condor*** from Johnson Diary passenger on the ***Beejapore***.

45. Health Officers Proforma Report on the ***Beejapore***.

46. Quarantine Burial Ground, Port Jackson.

Chapter 10 – The *Shackamaxon*

47. Ship ***Shackamaxon*** by Antonio Jacobsen.

48. Ship ***Shackamaxon*** lithograph by C.P. Williams.

49. Port Phillip 1853 by Thomas Kelly.

Chapter 11 – Conclusion

50. ***HMS Hercules*** Leaving Campbeltown Harbour, Scotland – Illustrated London News 15 January 1853.

51. Ship ***Dirigo***.

Introduction

I HAVE WRITTEN a number of books about emigration to the Australian colonies in the nineteenth century. In doing so, I have read of the experiences of individuals and families as told in diaries, journals, letters and newspaper reports. From around 1830, with the introduction of assisted passage arrangements, there had been a steady stream of people migrating to the colonies in vessels contracted by the Colonial Land and Emigration Commission (CLEC). The Commission acted on behalf of the colonies to identify and select suitable emigrants and to commission vessels to provide the transport.

The people selected as assisted emigrants were often people who had suffered traumas and deprivation. They frequently came from depressed parts of England, Scotland and Ireland. During the nineteenth century in the United Kingdom, the question of emigration arose for many people because of their deteriorating conditions and prospects in the community where they and their ancestors had lived, possibly for centuries. Leaving a small community of friends and relatives and travelling halfway around the world, with no prospect of return, is hard for me to comprehend. Most of those who came were not seafaring people, many would not previously have been onboard any type of vessel and most likely the majority would not have been able to swim. The thought of being confined on a small vessel in the ocean for several months must have been incredibly daunting. These people had provided the labour and the skills that contributed to the development and growth of the colonies in the first half of the century. They came in small ships accommodated beneath the main deck as steerage class passengers in crowded, noisy and smelly conditions. Although there was sickness on board during the long passage to the colonies, most of the emigrants arrived safely.

In writing about emigration to the colonies, I have examined the vessels used by the Emigration Commission. In this emigration story I have encountered the names of ships that clearly were used a number of times as carriers of emigrants. Some in fact made many trips to the colonies, which probably indicated that the Commission was satisfied with the arrangement and the vessel owners found it profitable. While the vessels varied in size, most of those engaged by the Commission in the first half of the century appeared to transport around 250 to 350 emigrants beneath the deck as steerage passengers.

The discovery of gold in Australia in 1851 had a profound effect on the colonies and on the lives of people living there, as well as on people living in the United Kingdom and in many other countries. It would be difficult to overstate the impact that occurred on the colonies—an impact that significantly changed the economic and social development for the remainder of the nineteenth century.

In the first three years of the gold rush, Australia received more free migrants from the United Kingdom than in the previous three decades of settlement. Most of those that came stayed to create the most affluent society the world had known to that date. The majority that came in that period paid their own fares and were the first significant group of paying passengers to choose to migrate to Australia rather than the United States.

A significant impact of the discovery of gold was the development of a set of social, cultural and economic opportunities in Australia that, for many, was not available in mid-nineteenth-century England and Europe or, for that matter, in late Qing Dynasty China. Hence, gold not only provided opportunities and moved the colonies away from dependence on wool and wheat, it created a new image abroad that helped distance the colonies from their penal origins.

By the end of 1852, 88,000 people had left the United Kingdom and arrived in the colonies (nine out of 10 went directly to Victoria). More ships sailed to Melbourne than to any other port in the world.

An enormous number of people moved quickly to the goldfields. Houses were deserted, businesses shut down and even some schools were closed. It was impossible to hire servants at any wage. Boats lay idle in the harbour because their masters were unable to keep their crew. Pastoralists were left without men. The shearing season had arrived, but the shearers had thrown their blades to prospect for gold and the Geelong stevedores, who customarily loaded the wool bales into ships' holds, had quit their jobs.

Many rural and urban employers in Victoria and the other colonies were left without labour. The pastoral lobby in Victoria was gravely concerned by the desertion of rural labourers and urged Lieutenant Governor La Trobe to urgently seek assisted immigrants to replace the agricultural workers that had deserted for the goldfields. This call for more assisted immigrants was echoed in the other colonies, as they had also lost large numbers of men to the Victorian goldfields. The effects of the gold rush were also being felt in the manufacturing towns of Yorkshire, which depended heavily on Australian wool.

The CLEC was under enormous pressure to keep the flow of assisted emigrants coming. However, they encountered a major impediment—a lack of vessels to transport them. The shipowners, normally commissioned by the CLEC, were not interested because they were making too much money transporting the hordes of paying passengers desperate to get to the goldfields. In looking at this problem and the vessels that were commissioned, the names of six ships emerged. They were very large, newly built North American clipper-style ships. Four were constructed in Canada and two in the United States. They had been designed to transport large amounts of cargo between North America and Liverpool.

They were magnificent-looking vessels that could be converted to transport twice as many passengers as the older style square-riggers that had transported many emigrants to the colonies in the first half of the century. Their availability was an answer to the problem that faced the Commission. Arrangements were quickly made to engage the six vessels to transport almost 5000 assisted passengers to the colonies of New South Wales, Victoria and South Australia in 1852.

Up until 1852, relatively few assisted emigrants failed to make it to their colonial destination. A small number lost their lives when their vessel was shipwrecked, often very close to their destination. Others died during the passage because of illness. Death from illness and disease during the voyage happened more frequently among children and infants. However, despite the existence of many endemic and epidemic diseases in Victorian Britain, most arrived successfully, able to start a new life and take advantage of opportunities in the colonies.

When I looked into the story of these six ships as transports of emigrants to the colonies, a very different story quickly emerged.

Liverpool, which was a very unhealthy place in the middle of the nineteenth century, wasn't the usual port of embarkation for emigrants going to Australia. In 1852, however, this is where the available vessels were based. Although these six magnificent-looking vessels were of the best design and could travel much faster than the normal emigration vessels, they were only able to transport such large numbers because they accommodated passengers in two decks below the main deck. The use of these very large ships out of Liverpool carrying so many people in very crowded conditions resulted in an enormous loss of life. The death rate among children and infants was particularly high.

In tracing the story behind each of these six ships, it became clear that a number of factors contributed to them becoming death ships. In telling this story, I have tried to identify the causes and their significance in what was a horrifying experience for many assisted emigrants selected for the colonies. In telling this story I felt it important for the reader to understand the pre-gold rush experience of emigrants, the nature of the diseases that existed in Victorian Britain, the significance of Liverpool as the port of embarkation and the urgency created by the gold rush. Almost 5000 emigrants set sail in these six ships for the colonies in 1852 and of those who arrived the experience was horrific.

Doug Limbrick

Chapter 1

EMIGRATING TO THE COLONIES

Far away – oh far away –
We seek a world o'er the ocean spray!
We seek a land across the sea,
Where bread is plenty and men are free,
The sails are set, the breezes swell –
England, our country, farewell! farewell

Anon

IT HAS BEEN estimated that over 1.5 million emigrants arrived in the Australian colonies from the United Kingdom during the nineteenth century. By the 1830s, when government-assisted passages commenced, almost 750,000 came as government emigrants.[1] An additional number were assisted in a variety of other ways through special schemes, assignment, sponsorship, indentured contracts and

---

1 Haines, R. & Shlomowitz, R. Nineteenth Century Emigration from the UK to Australia: An Estimate of the Percentage Who were Government Assisted. Flinders University, Working Papers in Economic History, No. 45, September 1990, p. 2.

bounty arrangements, which probably put the total number who were assisted to around one million. These passages were paid for by the colonies, largely using land sales to raise the necessary revenue. In the United Kingdom, the Colonial Land and Emigration Commission (CLEC, often referred to as the Emigration Commission or the Commission) managed the funds and organised the emigration arrangements on behalf of the colonies.[2]

The movement of people to the colonies increased significantly after the discovery of gold in 1851. Those who came in this period were largely people who paid their fare and were in a hurry to get to their destination. However, while this was happening, the movement of government-assisted emigrants continued. There were many working-class people and rural workers who were seeking a better life in the colonies and who could not afford the passage. Those who came with government assistance were referred to as emigrants. They were the ones that were prepared to take a risk and—while they came for a variety of reasons, with different hopes and aspirations—I believe they possessed those illusive and intangible qualities, which together produced the pioneer.

Emigrating to the Australian colonies from Britain during the nineteenth century necessitated a very long and difficult sea voyage. The emigrants came in various types of vessels, but for a significant part of the century this involved for most a voyage in a square-rigged sailing ship. According to Parsons, the average measurement of vessels carrying migrants from Great Britain and Europe to South Australia in the first 24 years of colonisation (i.e. from 1836) was about 450 tons, although some exceeded 1200 tons and some were as small as 100 tons or less.[3] Although steamships had been in existence since near the end of the eighteenth century, they had little impact on the Australian

---

[2] Note that a detailed account of the schemes of assistance and the role of the CLEC can be found in my book: *Farewell to Old England Forever*—particularly in Chapter 3.

[3] Parsons, Ronald. *Migrant Ships for South Australia 1836–1850*. Gould Books, Gumeracha South Australia, 1983 p. 13.

passenger trade until almost 100 years later in the latter part of the nineteenth century.

Square rigs allowed the fitting of many small sails to create a huge total sail area to drive large vessels. The alternative to a square rig was the fore-and-aft rig which involved the sails being attached along the same plane as the vessel's fore-and-aft line (i.e. the line of the keel). Fore-and-aft rigged vessels were generally more manoeuvrable and efficient when working in changing winds close to a coast. However, long ocean voyages required a large sail area to take advantage of the prevailing winds and current patterns. This was for many years the domain of the square-rigged vessel. On a square-rigged mast the sails had names that indicated their vertical position on the mast. The lowest square sail was the course, the next sail up the mast was called the topsail, and the next, the topgallant sail. Some vessels shipped a fourth sail above the other three called the royal.

The early convict and emigrant ships coming to the Australian colonies were blunt 'box like' wooden vessels. They were built with a flat bottom because of lack of docking facilities and so the vessel could rest on the mud in tidal rivers and harbours. Despite advances in ship design during the nineteenth century, these wooden sailing ships continued as regular passenger carriers until the 1860s and beyond. The nature and standard of service these vessels offered at the beginning of the period was much the same as that offered at the end.

One writer commented that these wooden vessels tended to ride like a cork on the great rollers of the Southern Ocean on their way from Cape Town to Australia. They shipped little water and in very bad weather they could drift more or less bow (front) on to the wind for days on end in relative safety.

In the nineteenth century the word 'ship' was only used to refer to a sailing vessel that was square rigged on all masts, that is, all masts carried yards (spars or cross pieces) with square sails. The ships had three or more masts—the foremast, the mainmast and the mizzenmast (back)—all rigged with square sails. These ships would usually carry fore-and-aft staysails between the masts. Some shipowners preferred vessels rigged as barques, which had the square sails on the mizzenmast replaced with sails carried fore and aft. The diagram below shows the difference in rigging.

Ship   Barque

Ship and Barque

There was little difference between the early naval ships and the emigrant ships. Many ships were used interchangeably as naval ships, convict ships and emigrant ships, with only some minor changes to the vessel's fittings.

Although for a few years during the gold rush there were many paying passengers, and some of them travelled cabin class, most people travelled to the colonies during the nineteenth century as steerage-class passengers. They were quartered beneath the decks where conditions were rudimentary, crowded, noisy, smelly and damp, and where they had little privacy. Throughout the nineteenth century, only about 10 per cent of passengers could afford to travel in cabins above the decks or under the poop deck (the elevated section) at the rear of the vessel.

The steerage area was normally fitted with many bunks down either side of the vessel with a long trestle table along the centre. The bunks were usually positioned so passengers lay in the same direction as the vessel (from fore to aft) but in some vessels the bunks were placed transversely (thwart ships). The latter caused passengers greater discomfort in rough seas. The best place to have a bunk was amidships because the rocking of the boat was felt less there. The bunks usually had straw mattresses or mattresses stuffed with straw. The headroom was usually between six and seven feet and was reduced in some areas because of the presence of large timber beams. These steerage areas were poorly ventilated and dark, and the conditions deteriorated in bad weather when the hatches had to remain closed (sometimes for days at a time). Under these closed-hatch conditions the smells were often overpowering because of seasickness, body odours, dampness, leaking water closets, whale oil in the lamps and from some types of disease (especially typhus which caused a very distinctive and pungent odour).

The steerage area of the vessel was immediately below the main deck and was also referred to as being between decks (shortened to 'tween decks) as it was located between the main deck and the lower areas used for storage and ballast. Although the origin of the expression 'steerage' is unclear, a number of sources agree it probably originated from the fact the control lines for the rudder ran on this level of the vessel.

'Emigrants at Dinner'.
Typical scene of steerage-class emigrants beneath the main deck.
(Illustrated London News, 13 April 1844)
[National Library of Australia]

For the passengers on this long voyage, it was sometimes an adventure, usually a challenge and often an ordeal. At times the voyage was also sheer boredom, with little to do in between the routine of shipboard life.

The conditions on board and the shipboard life for the majority of passengers and for the crew were spartan. As most of those who came to the Australian colonies travelled as steerage-class passengers, they were located where there was little space and privacy. Francis Taylor, a steerage passenger on the ***Stag*** travelling to Adelaide in 1850, commented:

… you cannot by day or night enjoy one moment of solitude…

I want a few days quietness, which I shall never get on the Stag …[4]

On some of the earlier passages, emigrants were exploited and subject to extremely primitive and unhealthy conditions. This exploitation led the British Government to take steps to protect those emigrating to the colonies. Regulations were gazetted and from around the 1840s greater protection was provided to emigrants on the Australian route. These regulations led to the development by the Emigration Commission of a lengthy set of rules and practices that had to be observed by all parties sailing to the Australian colonies.

One of the reforms involved the appointment of a surgeon superintendent for each passage. The person in this position was responsible for taking care of passenger welfare, providing for the spiritual wellbeing, setting and upholding the rules for the voyage, and acting as the disciplinarian as necessary. The surgeon superintendent, however, was not necessarily a person with any special medical qualifications and certainly was not a person with surgical qualifications in the modern sense. Some were not particularly competent and accepted the post to obtain free passage to the colonies. For others, this was a way of

---

4 Diary of Francis C Taylor transcribed and reproduced in Limbrick, Doug. The *Stag* Diary Passage to Colonial Adelaide 1850. Xlibris 2012 p. 96.

escaping financial or other problems at home. However, many were efficient and regulated life on board ship, particularly when conditions were difficult, discomfort high and sickness prevalent. Unfortunately, medical knowledge was such that little was known about the causes of the diseases that were prevalent on sailing vessels during this period. Even when they had some understanding of the cause of an illness, it was impossible to materially change the conditions on board these small sailing vessels (see Chapter 2 for further discussion on diseases and treatment). Thus, despite improved rules and practices, illness and death continued on board emigration vessels to the colonies. Although there were fewer incidences where surgeons followed the rules and were serious about their duties.

Given the deficiencies in selecting doctors for the emigration vessels, it is not surprising some were unable to perform the duties expected on the long passage to the colonies. On 7 January 1850 the *South Australian Register* reported the arrival of the **Brightman** and commented on the performance of the ship's doctor on the voyage out:

> *The Brightman, from Plymouth 17 September, with 120 passengers beside cargo, arrived at the Lightship on Saturday morning after a fine but lengthy passage of 110 days from the port of final departure. The passengers speak in highest terms of the Captain and general arrangements on board the Brightman, with one exception. The solitary exception alluded to, is the Doctor, whose conduct upon the voyage was anything but uniformly satisfactory. We forbear, at present, to publish the precise report as it has reached us, but seeing, as we have done, so many instances of very questionable appointment to the serious and important office of surgeon and surgeon superintendent, we cannot forego, the duty of advising those intending emigrants and confidential agents in England, who may read this announcement to make every possible enquiry.*

While there were accounts of incompetent doctors, there were also many positive experiences with very competent and compassionate doctors. The doctor on the **Stag**, William Thompson, was held in high regard by diarist and steerage-class passenger, Francis Taylor, during the 1850 voyage:

> *The surgeon, who is to every orderly passenger on board all that they could wish for, he truly spares no pains night or day in attending those who may require him professionally, whilst the healthy are treated more like brothers and sisters than total strangers.*[5]

While new regulations and requirements led to safer and cleaner conditions on board emigrant vessels, the physical environment produced by the weather and the state of development in sailing vessels meant emigration to the colonies under sail would continue to be a difficult and uncomfortable experience for most passengers. For example, seasickness was ever-present. It usually affected most passengers during the voyage. For some passengers it was a significant problem and for those it afflicted, the debilitation was very distressing. In these cases, the victims usually remained below deck for much of the voyage, emerging from time to time when conditions and strength allowed. This is illustrated in the following extract from the diary of Joseph Jennison on his 1853 voyage to Portland, Victoria, on board the **Marmion**:

> *We have had some dreadful weather since I wrote last. Seasickness is past description. We are ready to drop through want of food on the one hand and exertion of vomiting on the other. Five out of six in our mess have generally been sick at one time, so that even the few things we brought with us we cannot get them cooked. Putting our clothes on or carrying a little tub of water on deck when we are sick and the ship is rocking as though she were trying to go*

---

5   Diary of Francis C Taylor transcribed and reproduced in Limbrick, D. The Stag Diary Passage to Colonial Adelaide 1850. Xlibris, 2012, p. 66.

over, are undertakings of no mean importance, and more than once I have sat for an hour meditating the best way of performing these feats before I have begun.[6]

Travelling by cabin class did not prevent passengers experiencing seasickness. The captain of a square-rigger reported on the sight that greeted him after the first night at sea:

...I slept well, and was quite refreshed when I was called soon after dawn... the frightful aroma which filled the area assailed my nostrils... I realised that the crowd around me was vainly trying to cleanse itself . everybody and everything appeared to be permeated with the awful product of sea sickness. No one had been able to remain on deck during the night, as heavy sprays and occasional seas had apparently swept over the vessel, and the great conglomeration of people had all been herded close together in the crowded saloons. Some, by the very nature of things, had been sick, and the effect of these, in that confined space, had made everybody else follow suit. Never had I beheld so revolting a spectacle.[7]

Most emigrant vessels included children among their passengers. In fact, on some of the earlier voyages there were significantly more children than adults. Following a large number of deaths on some of these voyages, an enquiry recommended limiting the number of children and the complete exclusion of the very young. However, despite adopting these restrictions, it was common for pregnant women to embark and even give birth during the voyage. The birth of a child on land was a considerable risk at that time, but the risks to mother and child on board a vessel at sea were increased.

Apart from coping with a variety of sailing conditions, ranging from the doldrums in the tropics, to the gales of the Southern Ocean;

---

6   Diary of Joseph Jennison passenger on the Marmion 1853 in Morgan, Dalma and Poole, Henry. Voyage of a Lifetime. Adelaide, 1978, p. 55.
7   Hurst, A.A. The Call of High Canvass. London 1958, p. 52.

complying with the rules set by the surgeon superintendent, including the ship routine's daily and weekly timetable; the illness, seasickness, death and burials at sea and the occasional childbirth, the passengers to Australia had a considerable amount of spare time. For some passengers this meant long periods of boredom and some captains recognised the need to encourage activities to occupy the attention of passengers.

Sketches on Board an Emigrant Ship 1875
(Illustrated Australian News, 24 March 1875).
(State Library of Victoria)

On some vessels, the crew organised activities. However, on many voyages passengers were forced to make up their own entertainment to relieve the boredom. Card playing was a popular pastime and passengers could play under most conditions during the passage. When weather was favourable, passengers often tried to catch fish or dolphins. Encouraged by sailors, passengers also undertook bird 'fishing', using lines and hooks. A variety of birds followed the vessels at different points during the passage to the colonies. The largest was the albatross which could follow vessels for weeks during the passage through the southern hemisphere. According to seafaring tradition, it was bad luck to kill an albatross. However, many sailors ignored this and sought this big bird so they could make tobacco pouches from its big, webbed feet and pipe stems from the leg bones.

Books were usually at a premium on these long passages. Occasionally the surgeon superintendent had a small number, which they lent to selected passengers. On some passages the Bible was provided for the edification of passengers. Sometimes there were also Bible studies or Bible classes. For many of the passengers reading was not an option because of illiteracy and for those with books, reading conditions were often difficult below deck. Sometimes there were public readings of popular books of the day. Where a vessel was fortunate to have among its passengers two or three musicians, then this generally meant the voyage would pass more quickly because of concerts and dances organised up on the deck, weather permitting. Some used free time to write letters and think about family and friends left behind. A small number also kept a diary; usually intended as a means of letting family and friends know the details of the voyage.

The passage to the Australian colonies in the nineteenth century was the longest regular passage undertaken by sailing ships. The round trip or voyage frequently involved a journey that circled the world so the ships could use the prevailing winds. While it changed during the era of the sailing ship, the original route was over 13,000 nautical miles from England to Sydney. This course followed the route laid down by the Admiralty; used until the gold rush of the 1850s.

The voyage would start in the British Isles and, using the North Atlantic westerlies and then the northeast trade winds, the captain would seek to navigate the ship across the Bay of Biscay into the South Atlantic Ocean, where he would look for the southeast trade winds. These winds would carry the ship south towards the Roaring Forties, where the westerlies would speed the vessel towards Australia. The return trip would use the easterlies to Cape Horn, and after rounding the cape, would move north through the South Atlantic and then the North Atlantic Ocean to complete the circumnavigation.

However, the winds could not always be relied upon to arrive at the right time, from the right direction and in the right strength. It was not uncommon for vessels to spend weeks in the channel. They would often anchor waiting for a change of wind or, in case of too much wind, shelter at places like Plymouth.

Having at last departed, vessels often had considerable difficulty in crossing the Bay of Biscay. The weather in the bay can be very difficult for a modern liner to navigate, let alone a small timber vessel of less than 1000 tons. A different problem was encountered when ships approached the equator, where light winds could be expected. This was referred to as the doldrums and progress would be slow until the southeast trade winds were encountered. In fact, some vessels were becalmed, which frustrated a speedy voyage but offered opportunities for new experiences.

Many ships called at Madeira, Rio de Janeiro or Cape Town to repair storm damage and rest the crew. These stops also enabled passengers to recover and regain strength for the remainder of the passage. The captain also used these stopovers to replenish stores and water.

Until around the time of the gold rush to the Australian colonies, vessels on reaching Cape Town, would proceed to cross the southern Indian Ocean. At this point the passage was about half over. Around 7000 miles of ocean lay ahead devoid of any landmass, with nothing closer than India in the north and Antarctica in the south. While this part of the passage could be more difficult than what lay behind, the conditions were relatively mild compared to the southern route in later use.

A new route was devised by John Towson in 1847, examined by the admiralty and published as *Tables for facilitating the Practice of Great Circle Sailing*. The new route involved sailing as far south as ice would permit and eliminating Cape Town completely. Captain Godfrey, sailing the **Constance** (578 tons) in 1850, first tried it. Following the discovery of gold in the colonies there was an urgency to reach their destinations and many ships' masters wanted to follow the Towson route. This involved taking a large arc south towards the Antarctic and eventually swinging back towards Australia. This exploited the earth's round shape and the complete voyage out to the colonies and back to Britain became known as the Great Circle route.

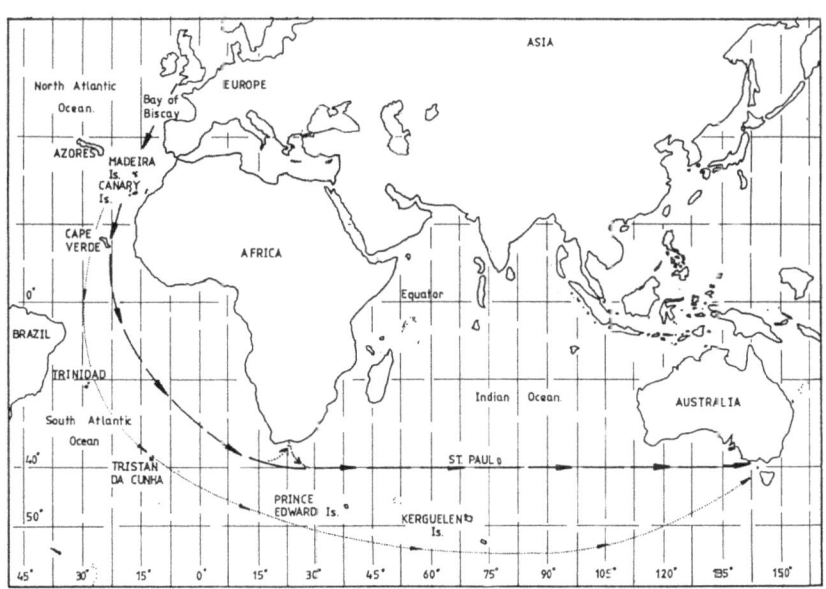

Map showing the two routes to the colonies

Note: The dark line and arrows mark the traditional route to the Australian colonies and New Zealand, while the lighter line marks part of the Great Circle route used increasingly after the 1850s.

The people of South Australia were clearly excited by the achievements of Captain Godfrey. The *South Australian Register* reported on 18 June 1850 on 'The Quickest Voyage to Australia – Great Circle Sailing':

Our accounts of Capt. Godfrey's unprecedented short voyage to South Australia, in the emigrant ship Constance, having produced a greater sensation among those interested in Australia and New Zealand than any voyage ever before made.

The Constance on her passage from Plymouth to Adelaide 1849 by T G Dutton
(Rex Nankivil Collection NK529, National Library of Australia)

Taking this route meant that vessels passed several hundred miles south of the Cape of Good Hope into seas that were frequented by icebergs. The small wooden square-riggers could easily be demolished if they collided with an iceberg. Even the larger composite or steel-hull sailing ships faced damage or destruction if a collision occurred. On this route, skillful sailing was needed to avoid the icebergs and because there were frequently extreme conditions, including gale force winds and gigantic seas. Sometimes it snowed and the crew often had to contend with ice on the deck, sails and rigging. This more southerly route usually meant sleepless nights for passengers, seasickness and a heightened fear of perishing at the hands of the sea. Many passengers were also not prepared for the extreme cold and were not dressed properly. With large waves breaking over the vessels, passengers were often wet and cold.

Sailing in a Big Seas – on Board the Loch Broom
(State Library of Victoria)

The seamen faced extreme conditions of hardship handling the sails in the southern latitudes. They had to be able to find every piece of rigging in the blackest of nights in gigantic seas with gale force winds blowing. Winds of 60 miles an hour were common, and the sails were often frozen stiff. For vessels sailing in the Great Southern Ocean this usually involved nights of extremely rough, cold and wet weather, which meant little rest for most passengers, especially any who were ill, who would experience many nights without sleep, damp, cold conditions, confinement under deck with closed hatches and considerable fear of perishing.

Diarist William Hewitt summarised his impressions of the passage on the ***Kent*** for the 300 passengers (approximately) that made the voyage in 1852:

> *Imagine 300 people, for the most part unaccustomed to the sea – imagine these people in their little crowded cabins overtaken [by] an earthquake, everything tossing and rolling around them, tins, clothes, boxes and pots... Overhead a thunder of waves, shouting, and bawling and shrieking as if the vessel was going down... Imagine amid all this a mass of human beings thrown in unusual, weltering confusion, sick to death and no one capable of helping another.*[8]

Ship *Red Jacket* Among the Icebergs
(State Library of Victoria)

---

8 Diary of William Hewitt 1852 onboard the Kent. Quoted in Walker, Mary Hewitt. Come Wind Come Weather. A Biography of Alfred Hewitt. Netley, South Australia, 1971, p. 26.

Most of the ships' masters had gained their sailing experience on the Atlantic. The much longer journey to Australia, including the long easterly run across the southern Indian Ocean, presented a problem that many had previously not encountered: the need to determine longitude.

In theory, the determination of longitude was a relatively simple matter: a sextant was used to determine the time on board ship and a chronometer, set at Greenwich time, was compared to time on the ship and the difference in hours and minutes was converted to degrees (each hour equalling 15 degrees, because every 24 hours involved one rotation of the earth through 360 degrees). However, they experienced difficulties when chronometers were too fast or too slow. To avoid this problem, several chronometers were needed, but as many masters were required to supply their own chronometers, they could generally only afford to provide one.

Latitude was also determined at noon, using the sunlight and a set of reference tables. Noon was thus an important time in the routine of shipboard life, as it was the time when the ship's time and position were fixed. In fact, the ship's day started at noon rather than at midnight. Prior to the use of chronometers, the early vessels used a sandglass to measure time. It took half an hour for the sand to run through and this was marked by the ringing of the ship's bell.

Even with these instruments, much of the navigation involved a calculated guess by the master. This was referred to as 'dead reckoning'. The instruments available to the master of a sailing vessel were fine in ideal conditions. Unfortunately, conditions at sea were rarely ideal, particularly in the southern latitudes. Following some weeks at sea, the chronometer could become inaccurate. Cloudy or overcast skies could prevent a master from taking sun or star sights with the sextant. The captain could never be certain how much sideways drift had occurred because of unknown currents.

Not only did the captain and crew of emigrant vessels need skill and luck to navigate when using the circle route after 1850, but considerable technical sailing skill was needed to safely get through the conditions likely to be encountered. For example, the ability to determine the correct amount of sail in heavy weather conditions was extremely important to the safety of the vessel. Without a sail a vessel could not be steered and would be at the mercy of the sea, but too much sail could have perilous results; the vessel being 'driven under', dismasted or capsized.

The *Stag* in a storm – watercolour by Alexander Weynton
(National Library of Australia)

The arrival of vessels was often fraught with difficulty because of the hazards associated with sailing along the long Australian coast. It's ironic to think that after safely navigating the difficulties of the vast oceans that the greatest peril could lie along the coast when the vessel was so close to its destination. There were many hazards along the coastline that led to the demise of convict and emigrant ships. Navigational technology at that time also meant that a captain would not be able to plot the position of the ship exactly. A vessel could easily be a few miles off course and this could be significant to the vessel's safety. Captain and crew, therefore, had to be alert and responsive until the vessel was finally anchored in harbour. All factors considered; it is amazing that so many small sailing vessels successfully made the long passage from the British Isles to the Australian colonies.

A passage to the Australian colonies in the nineteenth century was not a predictable proposition. The passage involved embarkation on a journey in a vessel that was small and uncomfortable, where there were considerable risks to passengers and crew, with weather that was unpredictable, where there were many unknowns, communications were primitive, the voyage was long and at times boring, many would be seasick and/or ill and some would die. What lay ahead on the passage to the colonies was a mystery for most passengers. This would have been the first experience of sea travel for many of the emigrants and so the realities of nineteenth-century sea life would have been a complete mystery. It's a little surprising that most emigrants arrived safely at their port of destination in the colonies.

As the vessels neared land, the decks would have been packed with passengers straining their eyes for that first sight of their new home. One wonders what they expected their new country to look like. I suspect they hoped that the first sight would reveal a land much like the one they had left behind. Letters and journals show that for many the first sight was marvellous, but for others it was a disappointment. Whatever the feeling about the view, there would have been a sense of relief in arriving safely and for most there would be no possibility of returning to Britain.[9]

---

9   Note: for a comprehensive account of the nineteenth-century emigration process see my book Farewell to Old England Forever. Publicious, 2017.

Bright Future 1852 by George Stafford
(State Library of Victoria)

As indicated in this chapter, the safe arrival of emigrants depended on many factors. One factor that could substantially increase the chances of a safe journey was elimination of exposure to disease. However, the people of nineteenth-century Britain were exposed to many diseases that were often spread because of the lack of adequate public health practices and knowledge about the cause of diseases and how they were transmitted. The state of medical knowledge also meant that if a disease was contracted, the outcome was not predictable and often resulted in death. Many of the diseases of the nineteenth century spread easily and rapidly in crowded situations, and the accommodation arrangements for steerage-class passengers described above involved emigrants sleeping and eating together in very close proximity over several months.

Chapter 2

EMIGRATION AND DISEASES OF VICTORIAN BRITAIN

Under the wide and starry sky,
Dig the grave and let me lie.
Robert Louis Stevenson[10]

HISTORY SHOWS IF the emigrants on a ship were healthy at the time of embarkation, then they would generally sail in a healthy vessel and the passage would be undertaken without any of the major problems associated with the diseases of the nineteenth century. Thus, those would-be emigrants that avoided exposure to the many diseases that prevailed in the nineteenth century had a greater chance of boarding in a healthy state. However, the prevailing conditions in Victorian towns and cities, including in the major emigration ports, were not conducive to nineteenth-century emigrants escaping exposure to, and

---

10 From the poem 'Requiem'. Stevenson died from tuberculosis, as did other poets including John Keats & Percy Shelly. It was almost fashionable in the 19th century for creative people, especially poets, to suffer from 'the lungs'.

possibly contracting, one of the diseases likely to be present in the local population.

It was, in fact, unhealthy to live in Victorian cities, though chances of illness and premature death varied considerably depending on who you were, where you lived, how much you earned, and how well you were fed. Social class and location mattered. Not all towns had equally high mortality rates and in some locations death rates in the countryside could match those in middle-class suburban areas of cities.

Bad housing, poor sanitation and overcrowding, which bred epidemic disease, were closely associated with inner-city areas. Ursula Henriques wrote:

> *In the first half of the nineteenth century no aspect of life suffered such cumulative deterioration as did public health.*[11]

Contemporary opinion was most concerned about infectious diseases. Even though more people died from 'other causes' than from all the infectious diseases combined. Diseases such as typhus and influenza were both endemic[12] and epidemic[13] and they killed large numbers of both rural and urban dwellers and greatly affected the young and malnourished of the urban slums. Smallpox became less important, in part because of the vaccination developed by Edward Jenner in the 1790s, even though it was not eradicated. Many people resisted the vaccination. There were rumours the vaccine could lead to people gaining bovine features.

---

11 Henriques, U. Before the Welfare State: Social Administration in Early Industrial Britain. Longman, 1979, p. 117.

12 A disease that constantly presents to a greater or lesser degree in people of a certain class or in people living in a particular location.

13 The rapid spread of infectious disease to a large number of people in a given population within a short period of time.

Emigration and Diseases of Victorian Britain 25

The Cow Pock, or the Wonderful Effects of the New Inoculation, cartoon by satirist James Gillray
(Wikimedia)

As towns grew, polluted water became an increasingly pressing problem and was the cause of many diseases, from infantile diarrhoea to typhoid fever and especially cholera.[14]

The Registrar General reported in 1841 that, while mean life expectancy in Surrey was 45 years, it was only 37 in London and 26 in Liverpool. The average age of 'labourers, mechanics, and servants' at the time of death was only 15. Mortality figures for crowded London districts like Shoreditch, Whitechapel and Bermondsey were typically twice as high as those for middle-class areas of London. Such statistics made people aware of the magnitude of disease, but also served as effective weapons for sanitary reformers when they brought their case before Parliament. Reports by the Poor Law Commission in 1838 and

---

14 Hardy, A. Urban Famine or Urban Crisis? Typhus in the Victorian City. Medical History, Vol. 32, 1988, pp. 401–425.

by several doctors, outlined causes and probable means of preventing communicable disease in poverty areas like London's Bethnal Green and Whitechapel.[15] A *Sanitary Report* in 1842 by Edwin Chadwick broadened the scope of inquiry geographically, as did a Royal Commission report in 1845 on the Health of Towns and Populous Places.

During the first decades of Victoria's reign, baths were virtually unknown in the poorer districts and uncommon elsewhere. Most households of all economic classes still used 'privy-pails'; water closets were rare. Sewers had flat bottoms, and because drains were made of stone, seepage was considerable. If, as was often the case in towns, streets were unpaved, they might remain ankle-deep in mud for weeks. For new middle-class homes in the growing manufacturing towns, elevated sites were usually chosen, with the result that sewage filtered or flowed down to the lower areas where the labouring populations lived. Some towns had special drainage problems. In Leeds, for example, the Aire River, fouled by the town's refuse, flooded periodically and sent noxious waters into the ground floors and basements of the low-lying houses. As Chadwick later recalled, the new dwellings of the middle-class families were scarcely healthier, for the bricks tended to preserve moisture. Even picturesque old country houses often had a dungeon-like dampness, as a visitor could observe:

> *If he enters the house, he finds the basement steaming with water-vapour; walls constantly bedewed with moisture, cellars coated with fungus and mould; drawing rooms and dining rooms always, except in the very heat of summer, oppressive from moisture; bedrooms, the windows of which are, in winter, so frosted on their inner surface, from condensation of water in the air of the room, that all day they are coated with ice.*[16]

---

15   Porter, D & Porter, R. Doctors, Politics and Society: Historical Essays. Rpodi, 1993, pp. 46–80.

16   Chadwick, Edwin. The General History of the Principles of Sanitation. Cassell & Company, 1889, p. 10.

In some districts of London and the great towns of England, the supply of water was irregular. Typically, a neighbourhood of 20 or 30 families on a particular square or street would draw their water from a single pump two or three times a week. Sometimes, finding the pump not working, they were forced to reuse the same water. When a local supply became contaminated, the results could be disastrous.

Diseases such as cholera, typhus, typhoid and influenza were more or less endemic, erupting into epidemics when the right climatic conditions coincided with periods of economic distress. The frequency of concurrent epidemics led people to believe one sort of disease brought on another; indeed, it was widely believed influenza was an early stage of cholera.

For much of the century, doctors were confused about the causes, course and treatment of typhus. The unpredictable behaviour of the severe contagions also intensified anxiety. They would appear, perhaps then subside for a month or two, only to reappear in the same locality or somewhere else. The individual sufferer had no way of predicting the outcome of the disease in their own case. The *London Medical Gazette* observed, during the 1833 epidemic, influenza patients 'might linger for the space of two or three weeks and then get up well, or they might die in the same number of days'. Just as frightening was the uncertain progress of typhoid. Infectious diseases were spatially concentrated: deaths from tuberculosis, typhus and cholera focused mainly on inner-city slum districts.

Tuberculosis

The main nineteenth-century killer of adults was tuberculosis. Few families were untouched by its effects and even in 1900 it was responsible for around 10 per cent of all deaths nationally, despite a significant decline from 1850.[17]

---

17 Thompson, T. Annals of Influenza or Epidemic Catarrhal Fever in Great Britain from 1510 to 1837. Sydenham Society, 1852, p. 289.

Tuberculosis (TB) was deemed the most deadly disease of its time and a particular threat to the working class. It was more prevalent in certain towns in Northern England than others and Lancashire was notorious for this disease.

TB is caused by the mycobacterium tuberculosis bacteria, which usually attack the lungs, but can affect almost any part of the body. What often appeared on a Victorian era death certificate was not TB but consumption, marasmus, phthisis, lung sickness, scrofula or King's evil (TB of the lymphatic glands), white swelling (TB of the bone) or Pott's Disease (TB of the spine).

Even by the end of the Victorian era, tuberculosis was the cause of a large number of all deaths per year. Despite this, the decline in TB over the period was great, particularly when paired with the improvements in public health, which were often credited to the regional Medical Officers of Health (MOH) who improved health care. The aims of the MOH were to increase the working class's confidence in hospitals and doctors while gradually altering their traditional beliefs and superstitions. From 1851 to 1870 there was a slight decline in the annual mortality from tuberculosis per thousand, but a rapid decline from 1870 until 1910. This is because most sanitary reforms and the majority of medical knowledge that influenced these reforms, occurred from 1870 onwards.[18]

Cholera

Cholera reached the shores of England in October 1831 when a ship carrying sailors who had the disease docked at Sunderland. This was the first outbreak of Asiatic cholera in Britain. From there the disease made its way north into Scotland and south toward London, eventually claiming 52,000 lives. It had taken five years to cross Europe from

---

18 Woods, R. Mortality Patterns in the Nineteenth Century. In Woods, R & Woodward, J (eds). Urban Disease and Mortality in Nineteenth Century England, London, 1984, pp. 37–64.

its point of origin in Bengal and by 1831 British doctors were aware of its nature, if not its cause. The progress of the illness in a cholera victim was a frightening spectacle: diarrhoea increased in intensity and became accompanied by painful retching; thirst and dehydration; severe pain in the limbs, stomach and abdominal muscles; and a change of skin hue to a sort of bluish-grey. The disease was unlike anything then known.

The impact of cholera was outlandish, unknown and monstrous. It seemed to recall the memory of the great epidemics of the Middle Ages, which invested it with a mystery and a terror that thoroughly took hold of the public mind. It brought tremendous ravages (so long foreseen and feared, but not explained); as it marched over whole continents; and it defied all the known and conventional precautions against the spread of epidemic disease.

Typhus

Not to be confused with typhoid fever (another common nineteenth-century killer), typhus is caused by the Rickettsia typhi or Rickettsia prowazekii bacteria. Spread by lice and fleas, typhus was a constant companion wherever overcrowding and poor hygiene existed. In the nineteenth century this could mean anywhere, but especially passenger ships, overcrowded cities and military camps. A military ancestor who died on a battlefield could have well been killed by typhus instead of by the enemy. According to the United States National Institutes of Health (NIH), untreated epidemic typhus (as opposed to endemic typhus) can kill 10 to 60 per cent of infected patients.

Hardest hit were the Irish. Typhus was one of the main causes of death during the nineteenth-century Irish Famine, wrote Dr Patrick Rowan in the *Irish Medical Times* on 28 October 2009. Six epidemics swept the isle in the 1800s, sustained by potato crop failure, primitive living conditions and poor hygiene.

When Irish emigrants set sail for North America, the lice and fleas travelled with them. Several memorials across North America mark where immigrants were contained while authorities tried to deal with typhus and prevent it from spreading into the general population.

During this period, death certificates relating to a death from typhus contained a range of terms, including typhus fever, malignant fever, jail fever (endemic typhus), hospital fever, ship fever, Irish fever, putrid fever, brain fever, bilious fever, spotted fever, petechial fever and camp fever.

Typhoid Fever

Typhoid fever is an acute illness caused by bacteria. It can also be caused by salmonella—a related bacterium that usually causes a less severe illness. For generations of physicians, typhoid was one of a broad class of fevers linked to putrid air. However, it occurs when the bacteria are deposited in water or food by a human carrier and then spread to other people in the area when they drink or eat the bacteria in contaminated food or water. The bacteria can survive for weeks in water or dried sewage. About 3–5 per cent of people become carriers of the bacteria after the acute illness. Others suffer a very mild illness that goes unrecognised. These people may become long-term carriers of the bacteria, even though they have no symptoms, and be the source of new outbreaks of typhoid fever for many years. Typhoid was also known as enteric fever and often improperly treated with purgatives; consequently, most sufferers died. It was not differentiated from typhus until the 1860s. Jacob Steere-Williams says of typhoid fever: 'typhoid was the pre-eminent 'filth disease' of the Victorian period'.[19]

Typhoid fever, unlike typhus, was no respecter of class, affecting both rich and poor alike.

---

19 Steere-Williams, Jacob. The Perfect Food and the Filth Disease: Milk, Typhoid Fever, and the Science of State Medicine in Victorian Britain, 1850–1900. Journal of the History of Medicine and Allied Sciences 65, 2010, p.13

Children and Nineteenth-Century Diseases

Given the low level of nutrition and the general squalor in many working-class homes, it's remarkable so many children survived their early years. Death was no stranger to working-class households in the first half of the nineteenth century and those deaths were often those of the children in the family. At the middle of the century, a quarter of all deaths in England and Wales were infants under one year of age, and children under five accounted for nearly half of all deaths. Babies were susceptible to infections resulting from contaminated food and the lack of personal cleanliness. Diarrhoea was common and could kill in 48 hours. Other illnesses that caused death in infants under two years of age were whooping cough, croup, measles and smallpox. Whooping cough could be deadly and in the mid years of the century it killed more females than males. In London it was responsible for more than one in 30 deaths and almost as many deaths as measles and smallpox combined.[20]

Measles is an endemic disease, meaning it has been continually present in a community, and therefore many people in the community develop a resistance. In populations not exposed to measles, exposure to this new disease was often devastating. This was a problem for people who were unexposed to urban diseases like measles and then moved from rural areas to urban areas to seek work, or to a port to emigrate. Because measles is a highly contagious disease that spreads easily, most people who are not immune and share a living space with an infected person will catch it. Measles did not decline in the nineteenth century and was most lethal in the age group from six months to two years.

Scarlet fever was an acute infection of the throat, skin and middle ear. It mainly affected children under 10 years old, with a much higher fatality rate in infants. A dramatic fall in mortality took place in the latter years of the nineteenth century.

---

20 Hopkins, Eric,. Childhood Transformed. Working class children in nineteenth century England, Manchester Press, 1994, p.113

While diphtheria was a significant cause of death among children, it was not classified until 1861. Before then it was thought to be scarlet fever due to the uncertainty in diagnosis. Caused by airborne bacteria, it could also be transmitted through milk and on clothing and objects. It affects the throat, but also produces toxins that can cause permanent damage to the heart and nervous system.

While croup affected small babies, it was not a major killer and disappeared when teething began.

Among older children, the principal deadly diseases were scarlet fever, measles, diphtheria and smallpox.

The 1848 edition of *Buchan's Domestic Medicine* (a popular treatise on the cure and prevention of diseases), had a frontispiece showing the symptoms of smallpox, scarlet fever and measles, and it listed among the general causes of illness 'diseased parents', night air, sedentary habits, anger, wet feet and abrupt changes of temperature. The causes of fever included injury, bad air, violent emotion, irregular bowels and extremes of heat and cold.

Treatments relied heavily on a 'change of air', together with emetic and laxative purgation and bleeding by cup or leech (a traditional remedy only abandoned in the mid-century) to clear 'impurities' from the body. Only a very limited range of medications were available. The approach to treatment adopted by doctors in the nineteenth century was described by Bryson as follows:

> …*until well into the nineteenth century most doctors approached diseases not as distinct afflictions, each requiring its own treatment, but as generalised imbalances affecting the whole body. They didn't give one drug for headaches and another for, say, ringing in the ears, but rather endeavoured to bring the whole body back into a state of equilibrium by purging it of toxins through the administration of cathartics, emetics, and diuretics or by relieving a victim of a bowl or two of blood.*[21]

---

21 Bryson, Bill. The Body. A Guide for Occupants. Doubleday, 2019, pp.131-2.

The power of prayer was regularly invoked by those who were afflicted or by family or friends. Parents often resorted to superstitious practices derived from folk medicine—such as taking a child for a ride on a donkey (associated with Jesus) or having a frog breathe into the child's mouth— to relieve the suffering of their children.

As many of the diseases of the nineteenth century were highly contagious and many were endemic and epidemic, a nineteenth-century emigration vessel, with large numbers of passengers in a crowded environment, would have provided ideal conditions for the spread of these types of diseases. Confronted with them at sea, a doctor would have a limited number of options for treating a sick individual, let alone in dealing with a mass outbreak of one or more of these diseases.

The Irish emigrated to North America in large numbers fleeing poverty, disease and famine and many died during the passage due in part to the conditions on board. The term 'coffin ship' was used to refer to those that carried Irish immigrants, particularly during the Great Irish Famine and Scottish highlanders displaced by the Highland Clearances. A coffin ship was often a vessel in poor condition overloaded and over insured so it was more valuable to its owners if it sunk.

Coffin ships carrying emigrants, crowded and disease-ridden, with poor access to food and water, resulted in the deaths of many people as they crossed the Atlantic, and led to the 1847 North American typhus epidemic at quarantine stations. There were no government schemes of subsidised or free passage for those emigrating to North America (unlike emigration to the Australian colonies from around 1830). While coffin ships were the cheapest way to cross the Atlantic, mortality rates of 30 per cent were common. It was said sharks could be seen following the ships because so many bodies were thrown overboard.

Legislation to protect emigrant passengers, the Passenger Vessels Act, was first enacted in Britain in 1803 and continued to evolve in the following decades. A revised Act in 1828, for example, marked the first time the British government took an active interest in emigration matters. Within a few years, regulations were in force to determine the maximum number of passengers a ship could carry, and to ensure sufficient food and water be provided for the voyage.

But the legislation was not always enforceable, and unscrupulous shipowners and shipmasters found ways to circumvent the law. In addition, ships sailing from non-British ports were not subject to the legislation. As a consequence, thousands of emigrants experienced a miserable and often dangerous journey. By 1867, regulations were more effective, thus providing people with the promise of a safe, if not comfortable, voyage.

Ill health was a problem on board many immigrant ships of the nineteenth century, particularly among working-class passengers. They lived below deck in the steerage area, where it was dark, damp, cramped, and often crawling with vermin. As well as lice, there were usually ticks, cockroaches and rats. Poor hygiene made things worse for these passengers and sometimes there was an outbreak of serious disease—measles, diphtheria, scarlet fever, typhoid, smallpox and tuberculosis could all strike on voyages undertaken by emigrants seeking a better life in North America or the colonies in Australian or New Zealand.

Most of the emigrants who went to North America departed from Liverpool, while those who emigrated to the Australian colonies and to New Zealand departed from several ports, including Liverpool. Departures from this location usually involved emigrants spending time in the city prior to embarkation, which exposed them to those diseases present in the Liverpool population and those that were carried by people arriving there.

Many of the nineteenth-century diseases were spread between countries by the movement of people. Many of the diseases were endemic in Britain and were taken to the Australian colonies with the emigrants.

While measles was endemic in Britain during the early 1800s, it seems from Australian government records measles was only introduced after 1850, despite regular shipping contact between the two countries. The early absence of measles was remarkable as diphtheria, scarlet fever and whooping cough exacted a great toll on European settlers and Aboriginal Australians in early colonial times following the first fleet to Australia in 1788. It has been suggested by Paterson et al. that:

> *Australia was initially protected against measles because of its high infectivity with outbreaks possibly burning out during the voyage to Australia, which could take up to 8 months.*[22]

It seems this changed from around 1850 with the use of some faster vessels, particularly the North American clipper-style ships, accompanied by the move towards using the faster Great Circle sailing route. The increase in the number of children emigrating also contributed to the arrival of measles and its establishment as an endemic disease in the populations of the Australian colonies.

As Liverpool was a major port in the emigration process during the nineteenth century, the prevailing conditions; the arrangements for processing, assisting and supporting emigrants while there; and the living arrangements on board the vessels, were all important in determining the health outcomes for emigrants during their voyage to their destination, particularly during the relatively long passage to the Australian colonies.

---

22 Paterson, B.J, Kirk, M. D, Cameron, A. S, D'Este, K. S, Durrheim, D. Historical data and modern methods reveal insights in measles epidemiology: a retrospective closed cohort study. BMJ Open, BMJ Publishing Group, Vol 3, Issue 1, 2013.

Chapter 3

EMIGRATING FROM LIVERPOOL

Farewell, England! Blessings on thee –
Stern and niggard as thou art.
Harshly, mother, thou hast used me, And my bread thou hast
refused me: But 'tis agony to part.

Anon

FROM THE FOURTEENTH century, Liverpool started to develop and prosper. It progressively established its reputation as a trading port, importing mainly animal skins from Ireland, whilst exporting both iron and wool. Prosperity followed the increasing trade.

This growth and prosperity was, in the main, paid for by the infamous triangular trade of sugar, tobacco and slaves between the West Indies, Africa and the Americas. Being strategically placed to exploit such transatlantic trade, Liverpool soon became the fastest growing city in the world.

The newcomers—arriving mainly from Ireland and Wales—were

forced to live in dreadful conditions, with overcrowded houses that lacked sewers.

Liverpool's Old Dock was built in 1715 and was the world's first enclosed commercial dock. The Lyver Pool, a tidal inlet in the narrows of the estuary, was converted to create it. Further docks were added in the eighteenth century and eventually all were interconnected by lock gates, extending 7.5 miles along the Liverpool bank of the River Mersey. From 1830 onwards, most of the building stone was granite from Kirkmabreck, near Creetown, Scotland. Liverpool grew to be the third largest port in the country, behind London and Bristol. As the nearest port to Manchester, Liverpool also benefited from the growth of the Lancashire cotton industry. Liverpool was also the main port for receipt of timber from North America. Canada Dock was opened in 1859 when Canada was Britain's major source of timber. Around that time sailing ships often crowded the dock as hordes of workers unloaded tons of wood which was transported away by horses and stacked neatly on the quaysides. Many of the timber carrying ships were very large and specially built in North America for the timber trade (six such vessels are the main subject of this book). The image below from a painting by artist Robert Dudley presents an atmospheric view of Canada Dock vividly capturing the hustle and bustle of the port. The number of horses in the painting underlines the importance of horse-drawn carts in carrying goods from docks to warehouses.

Canada Timber Docks, Liverpool, Towards Close of Day, by Robert Dudley
(Merseyside Maritime Museum)

The interconnected dock system was the most advanced port system in the world. This enabled ship movements within the dock system 24 hours a day, isolated from the high River Mersey tides. Parts of the system are now a World Heritage Site.

The latter part of the eighteenth century in the county of Lancashire was marked by a rapid population growth of many of its towns and cities as a result of industrialisation and urbanisation. In fact, the proportionate population growth in the county surpassed that of the other counties in England. The overall expansion of Liverpool and Manchester largely contributed towards this, but even with the exclusion of these cities, the county still ranked third in growth from 1790 onwards.[23]

By 1851 the population of Liverpool reached more than 300,000,

---

23   King, S & Weaver, A. Lives in Mary Hands: The Medical Landscape in Lancashire 1700–1810. Medical History 2000, No. 45. pp. 173–200.

many of these included Irish immigrants who were fleeing the potato famine of the 1840s.

By the 1860s, the manufacturing industry was booming, particularly in such areas as shipbuilding, rope making, metalworking, sugar refining and machine making.

Life was a terrible ordeal for those people of Liverpool who were forced to live in the overcrowded, disease-ridden, filthy parts of the city. Conditions were worst in the central areas.

Dr Trench, the Liverpool Medical Officer of Health (MOH), noted the attention of the Health Committee was always occupied with problems like 'the number of poor, especially of Irish and other destitute immigrants, promiscuously collected in certain squalid localities; filth and penury pent up in airless dwellings'.[24] Overcrowding and ill-ventilated courts and alleys were common and the construction and position of middens and cesspools were all risk factors that led to infection. Privy middens were open holes leading to cesspools, which could flood. The city authorities gradually replaced them with pail middens (an early form of dry toilet that relied on regular collection), and eventually water closets.

Diseases occurred where there was poverty, overcrowding, bad ventilation and filth, and many areas of Liverpool provided the ideal conditions. The Annual Report of the MOH for 1864 commented on the increased level of poverty in the town, stating, with regards to assisting those in poverty, 'the amount disbursed from 25 June to 10 December 1864 was, within a few pounds, double that in 1863. There were 1061 more persons relieved than those in 1863 over the same months'.[25] Dr Trench believed the major cause of indigence was insufficient work for the unskilled labourer. Casual labour was more prevalent in Liverpool

---

24 Trench, William S. Report on Defects in Midden System, Liverpool Health Committee ,1863. Liverpool Records Office.
25 Ibid

than in many other major towns due to the number of workers employed in the dock industry. This work was not regular as it was subject to the number of ships arriving at the port. Trench said of these people, 'their ragged, insufficient clothing indicates that indigence was of a long continuance'.[26]

The appalling housing conditions in Liverpool in the nineteenth century were the perfect habitat for lice. They could be killed by disinfecting patients and dwellings, which usually ensured the disease did not spread. The typhus problem was particularly acute in lodging houses. Dr Trench was a member of the Deputation appointed to inspect the 'Common and Model Lodging Houses and Model Dwellings for the working classes of the Metropolis'. In his letter, which was read to the Lodging House Committee in Liverpool, he pointed out the space allocated per individual per room, as advised by the Secretary of State, was much more than found in Liverpool. On informing his inspector that in London the rule was 400 cubic feet per adult as the legal space of a sleeping room, he remarked, in many rooms in Liverpool the mother would not only have to separate from her infants but would have to leave the husband halfway out on the stair. The same regulations applied to sublet houses in Liverpool, and the sharing of sleeping accommodation and the mixture of the sexes in many houses appalled Trench. Up to six adults in a room of 600 cubic feet was very common.[27]

Cholera was a disease that exposed the insanitary conditions in which the majority of Liverpool's population lived in the mid-nineteenth century. It also exposed the risks taken by the Irish poor to maintain their cultural traditions, despite advice from Trench as MOH. The disease reached epidemic proportions in the second half of 1866.

There was concern at the time about the practice of 'wakes' because

---

26 Ibid.
27 Annual Report of the Medical Officer of Health for Liverpool, 1866.

they involved leaving the body of the deceased in the home. Lots of families lived and slept in single rooms and this meant they were sometimes forced to retain in their homes the bodies of those who had died from smallpox or other diseases. It was not until 1871, with an epidemic of smallpox raging in the town, that the Council decided to provide a mortuary for bodies dead from infectious disease. The Council purchased a hearse, obtained contracts for the purchase of coffins and took on the management of the removal of bodies to the mortuaries once they'd received a certificate from the MOH and an order from the Justices. At the same time, the Council voted £5000 towards the erection of a hospital for infectious diseases in Everton.

Victorian Liverpool was clearly not a healthy place and this was significant in the context of the city's role as the gateway to the New World for so many who were seeking to emigrate.

Liverpool's history is bound to the tides of transatlantic transportation: from the city that grew powerful and prosperous from the slave trade, it moved to play an important role as the port of departure for millions of people seeking new lives in the New World countries of USA, Canada, Australia and New Zealand. Passengers, some of whom were emigrants or indentured servants, were carried regularly to North America and the West Indies from about 1660 onwards. In the nineteenth century, thousands of emigrants from the British Isles and mainland Europe left from Liverpool. The establishment of regular sailing packet lines from 1818 and the huge demand for North American timber and cotton as raw materials for British industry led to well-established transatlantic links, and emigrants, along with British manufactured products, provided a useful return cargo.

Such were the numbers of emigrants, that it has been estimated between 1830 and 1930 over nine million emigrants sailed from Liverpool bound for a new life in the USA, Canada, Australia and New Zealand. For much of this period Liverpool was, by far, the most important port of departure for emigrants from Europe because, as well as its established transatlantic links, Liverpool was well placed to receive the many emigrants from the countries of north-western Europe. These emigrants included Scandinavians, Russians and Poles, who crossed the North Sea to Hull by steamer and then travelled to Liverpool by train. Irish emigrants crossed to Liverpool by steamship, and the Irish potato famine of 1846–1847 further increased the demand for passage from Liverpool. By 1851 it had become the leading emigration port in Europe, with 159,840 passengers sailing to North America, as opposed to the second largest port, Le Havre (northern France), with 31,859. In the same period a large number of emigrants departed from Liverpool to join the gold rush in Australia. But this traffic, together with emigrants to New Zealand, which began to grow in the 1860s, was shared with other UK ports of Southampton, London and Plymouth.[28]

Georges Dock Liverpool
(Merseyside Maritime Museum)

---

28 McIntyre-Brown, A. & Shaw, F. Connections: Liverpool Global Gateway. Garlic Press Publishing Ltd., 2005, pp.56-57.

Liverpool is the birthplace of the famous Cunard Line. The Company's first ship, **Britannia**, departed from its Liverpool headquarters on her maiden voyage to Boston on 4 July 1840. The White Star Line—owners of the **Titanic** and founded in 1845—was also based in Liverpool, and vessels from several other shipping lines also departed from here.

The first task of the emigrants arriving in Liverpool, if their passage had not previously been paid for by friends or relatives in the country of destination or through a charity or government-assisted passage scheme, was to make the best bargain they could with the passenger-brokers and pay their passage money. The competition in this trade was great, and fares could vary from day to day, and even from hour to hour, particularly for those travelling to North America.

The walls of Liverpool were covered with notices relating to the availability of ships sailing from Liverpool, for which many firms acted as passenger-brokers, and each notice set forth in large letters the excellent qualities of the vessels the brokers represented.

Emigrants were generally not allowed on board their ships until the day before sailing, or sometimes the day of sailing, so this meant most spent between one and 10 days waiting for their ship in a Liverpool lodging house. Sometimes they spent longer periods waiting to set off on their ship because journeys were at the mercy of the weather. In the mid-nineteenth-century, emigrants passing through Liverpool were liable to harassment and fraud by local confidence tricksters, known as 'runners' or 'man catchers'. The runners frequently snatched their victims' luggage and would only return it if they paid a fee. The man catchers often worked with lodging houses, which in the 1850s were often inhospitable, dirty and overcrowded, and received a commission from agents employed by shipping lines. The following account from the *London Times* on 11 May 1850 illustrates the problems faced by emigrants:

> **MAN-CATCHING IN LIVERPOOL** – *A few months ago some*

of the more respectable firms connected with the emigrant trade of this port resolved to dispense with the services of the passenger agents, who had been previously in receipt of commission from their offices for the passengers whom they secured. These passenger agents have obtained a rather disreputable notoriety, and are, now popularly known by the designation of "man-catchers", and so glaringly dishonest were their practices, and so unequivocal was the condemnation pronounced against the system by Government and local authorities, that the more respectable shippers at this port at the period referred to, met and resolved not to employ "man-catchers" for the future. Whether the agreement entered into was ever strictly observed we know not, but up to a very recent date it was not openly broken through. Now, however, the mask is thrown away, and the system of "man-catching", with all its attendant evils, flourishes in all its "rank luxuriance"; emigrants are fleeced in every possible shape, and after the most approved fashion, and those who fleece them receive a bonus when they have "plucked the pigeons" to hand them over to the emigration-offices…

Meetings were held by Liverpool citizens concerned about the welfare of the emigrants. The following report in the *London Times* on 7 May 1850 is typical of the efforts to improve ways of protecting emigrants:

PROTECTION OF EMIGRANTS – LIVERPOOL, Monday.
– A large and influential meeting of clergymen, merchants, and others was held at the Clarendon rooms today, to take into consideration a proposition for providing an emigrants' home in Liverpool. The Venerable Archdeacon Brooks occupied the chair, and several addresses were delivered showing the necessity for the establishment of such an institution as the one proposed. Lieutenant Hodder, the Government emigration agent, stated that when the Irish emigrants landed at the Clarence-dock, of this port, they were beset by a body of men banded together, who were known as the "forty thieves", the most unscrupulous set of scoundrels that could

possibly be conceived. These men acted as porters and handed the poor emigrants over to "land sharks", who obtained a percentage from the passenger-brokers for each customer they obtained. The lodging-house keepers and provision-dealers also gave a further commission to these unprincipled agents; and the emigrants were plundered on all sides to the greatest extent. He characterised the emigration system as one vast combination of fraud, with the most extensive ramifications.... The Rev. H. McNiele moved a resolution to the following effect: - "That this meeting, feeling the great influence that emigration has on this country, as well as on the colonies, deem it of the utmost importance that measures, should be taken for the protection of the emigrants, and for the improvement of their temporal and moral conditions, especially in this great port of Liverpool." This motion was unanimously agreed to, and a committee was appointed to devise a plan, it being the general opinion that one large building should be fitted up for the emigrants, and that such an institution would not only be self-supporting when once established, but would afford the emigrants greater comforts and much greater advantages, at much smaller cost, than those they at present derive from the doubtful sources which are open to them.

Many of those who came to Liverpool in order to emigrate to the New World came from poor rural communities where they had experienced poverty and sometimes eviction and dispossession. It's clear many of those arriving were traumatised, malnourished and possibly uncertain about the decision to emigrate. Hence Liverpool was not only unsafe and unhealthy but also a cultural and ethnic melting pot with large numbers arriving from many of the depressed parts of England, Scotland, Ireland and Eastern Europe.

Recognising emigrants required some support and protection the Liverpool Port Authority, in 1851, gave serious consideration to building a special emigrant depot close to the Irish steamer terminal at Clarence

Dock, with accommodation for 4000 people at a time. The depot was never built, but one was opened for emigrants departing for Australia at Birkenhead in 1852. This was the fourth and last depot established by the CLEC to assist passengers leaving Britain for the Australian colonies. The others were at Plymouth, Southampton and Deptford (near London). They were largely contained in adapted boarding houses and were fairly small. Birkenhead was larger and established in a warehouse built for the shipping trade but never used for that purpose. It wasn't until late in the nineteenth century most emigrants were able to stay in lodging houses owned or supervised by shipping companies.

The Embarkation, Waterloo Docks, Liverpool[29]
(State Library of Victoria)

Even with access to a depot, passengers were exposed to crowded town life on arrival in Liverpool. The depot could only accommodate 400 at a time and so it wasn't uncommon for some passengers to spend more time in squalid, overcrowded lodging houses. Even respectable

---

29 *Illustrated London News,* 6 July 1850, p. 17.

establishments frequently offered only boards to sleep on – and no blankets. The depot at Birkenhead involved exposure to a crowded environment much like the environment emigrants were about to experience on board ship. The sleeping arrangements involved a large room on the first floor with single men sleeping on one side, single women on the other side and families in between. Communal eating occurred on the ground floor. These arrangements meant infectious diseases could be easily passed on among the passengers while in the emigration depot.

Birkenhead Depot Ground Floor – Communal Eating
(National Library of Australia)

The feeling uppermost in the minds of many thousands of the poorer class of British emigrants, when the cheers of the spectators and of their friends on shore proclaimed the instant of departure from the land of their birth, must have been a mixture of sadness and excitement. The Irish emigrants must have had a similar feeling, though possibly less intense, and could scarcely fail to be excited. Little time, however, was left for the emigrants to indulge in these reflections. The ship was towed by a steam-tug five or 10 miles down the Mersey, and during the time occupied in traversing these 10 miles, two very important processes were carried out: a search for stowaways followed by a roll call of the passengers. Many departing for the Australian colonies shared these experiences and the number increased substantially after gold was discovered in 1851.

Quarter Deck of an Emigrant Ship – the Roll Call
(*The Illustrated London News*, 1850, v. 17, p. 20.)

Chapter 4

LA TROBE, THE GOLD RUSH AND THE DEMAND FOR LABOUR

A complete mental madness appears to have seized almost every member of the Community.

Bathurst Free Press, 17 May 1851

FROM 1849, THE gold rush in California had attracted thousands of Australians. Prior to this time there was no interest in New South Wales in supporting exploration for gold in the colony, as it was feared a discovery would lead to social and economic dislocation. However, the loss of so many men from the colony led Governor FitzRoy to offer a generous reward for anyone who discovered a commercially viable deposit in New South Wales. The reward was claimed by Edward Hargraves, who had returned from an unsuccessful time on the Californian goldfields.

The rush was now on and men from all vocations became gold miners and headed for Summer Hill Creek. They carried with them digging implements of every kind, as blacksmiths couldn't keep up with the demand for picks. Prices for basic commodities doubled overnight. FitzRoy, being afraid of the impact on the colony, imposed a miner's tax of 30 shillings a month to be paid regardless of whether the prospector found gold or not. He reasoned that the unsuccessful miners would quickly return to their former employment, as they would not be able to afford to pay the tax without a source of income.

The discovery quickly had an impact on the colony—particularly on prices and the availability of labour for rural and other industries.

> *In Sydney, labourers' pay rose from 17 or 20 shillings a week to 48 shillings. Clerks complained that their meagre pittances could not support them since the price of groceries had risen 50 per cent almost overnight. They must either get more pay or join the rush.*[30]

The discovery of gold in New South Wales disturbed those in the newly independent colony of Victoria. Late in May 1851 the startling news of the gold rush over the Blue Mountains in New South Wales reached Port Phillip. Distance and the wintery weather deterred many, but within a couple of weeks at least 200 men had packed a swag and departed on the three week trudge to the Bathurst area of New South Wales. It's likely as many as 1000 joined the rush overland or by sea.

It was feared Victorians would continue to desert the new colony in large numbers and join the gold rush in New South Wales. To counter this, in June 1851 Lieutenant Governor Charles La Trobe offered a reward of £200 for the discovery of gold within 200 miles of Melbourne. William Campbell had discovered gold north of Ballarat in 1850 but did not disclose the discovery until a month after La Trobe had offered the reward. The Victorian gold rush was now on.

---

30 Monaghan, Jay. The Australians and the Gold Rush. University of California Press, 1966.

La Trobe, the Gold Rush and the Demand for Labour   53

Bright Visions or the Gold Diggings created by George Stafford
(State Library of Victoria)

The rush to the diggings by large numbers of people from many different vocations was reported by a correspondent in the Victorian town of Buninyong in the *Argus* (Melbourne) 8 October 1851:

> *Day by day, hour by hour, the population increases and concentrates at Ballarat, a population who appear at the same time, merely as heralds of coming multitudes. We are thousands, and our tents may be numbered by the hundred, our huts and mia mias by fifties. Men flock to Ballarat, as did the tribes of old to Rome. Drays and carts, equestrians and men on foot, M.L.C's, Bank Directors, Captains of Vessels, Aldermen, Common Councilmen, Lawyers, Doctors, every grade of man down to him who carries a swag, pour in upon us —battalions of tin dishes glint in the sunshine, brigades of picks emerge from the ranges and gullies, regiments of shovels and troops of crowbars deploy from the forests,*

and take up their stations in array for gold-digging, make their preparations, and bivouac for the night. The roads are lined with encampments, the trees are felled in every direction, and the route marked by the nightly watch fires of the adventurers. A vast concentration is taking place, where a community of interest, after a pause, will create a community of feeling, and before the lapse of a twelvemonth the gold diggers of Victoria will be the most powerful class in the province, in numbers, and in wealth, which still flows in at high-tide prosperity.

There were certainly some prophetic words contained in that report in the *Argus*; those who went to the diggings had a considerable impact on the development of the social, economic and cultural shape of Victoria and Australia.

Gold Washing Fitz Roy Ophir Diggings 1851 by George Francis Angas
(State Library of Victoria)

However, the immediate impact was the significant disruption that concerned the lieutenant governor, who saw negative consequences for the colony. He reported the mayhem to the Secretary to the Colonies, Earl Grey, in a letter dated 10 October 1851, which included the following remarks:

> *It is quite impossible for me to describe to your Lordship the effect these discoveries have had on the whole community. Within the last three weeks the towns of Melbourne and Geelong and their large suburbs have been in appearance almost emptied of many classes of their inhabitants; the streets which for a week or ten days were crowded by drays loading with the outfit for the workings are now seemingly deserted.*[31]

La Trobe's letter did not exaggerate the impact. Houses were deserted, businesses shut down and even some schools were closed. It was impossible to hire servants at any wage. Boats lay idle in the harbour because their masters were unable keep their crew. Pastoralists were left without men. The shearing season had arrived, but the shearers had thrown their blades to prospect for gold and the Geelong stevedores, who customarily loaded the wool bales into ships' holds, had quit their jobs. La Trobe feared the new colony might parallel California in crime and disorder. On 15 August he followed the precedent set by Governor FitzRoy and asserted the Crown's right to all gold in Victoria, thus inaugurating a licence system similar to that used in New South Wales.

The introduction of a miner's tax didn't stop the movement to the goldfields. La Trobe panicked and threatened to double the monthly impost. A series of large meetings and rowdy protests followed, and La Trobe backed down. The *London Times* of 22 December 1851 reported this as La Trobe having been '… humbled in the dust before a lawless mob'.

---

31   Further Papers Relative to the Recent Discovery of Gold in Australia. British Parliamentary Papers, 1852 contained in Victorian Parliamentary papers GP V 1851/52 p. 257–64.

These protests from the goldfield were about much more than the licence fee and as discontent continued to simmer, it coalesced into a more far-reaching set of popular grievances and demands for universal male suffrage.

A booming wool industry and the arrival of many immigrants as a result of assisted passage had given Victoria a solid economic base by the time gold was discovered. The rush from overseas that followed was, in time, to have an enormous impact on the growth and the shape of Victoria and the other colonies. On the goldfields there was a high degree of uniformity and a process of social change that tended to invert the social order experienced in Britain and Europe. The *Argus*, on 7 August 1852, reported this levelling effect in a humorous way, describing a patron at an inn on the way to the goldfields who thought 'that all our neighbours would be gentry; Oh! No, Jack's as good as his master here; you elbow fellow'. This social transformation, which has been linked to the goldfields, was described by anthropologist Victor Turner as being characterised by:

> *the suspension of the usual norms and social roles, and by an overflowing sense of communitas or collective camaraderie.*[32]

The discovery of gold led to the development of a set of social, cultural and economic opportunities in Australia that, for many, was not available in mid-nineteenth-century England and Europe or, for that matter, in late Qing Dynasty China. Hence, gold not only provided opportunities and moved the colonies away from dependence on wool and wheat but created a new image abroad that helped distance the colonies from their penal origins. The change in image helped foster one that depicted the colonies as places of opportunity and wealth, employment and commerce. This made emigration to the colonies even more attractive and helped create an era of mass migration from all over the world. The gold rush was not just one of gold but of

---

32 Turner, V and Bruner, E. M. The Anthropology of Experience. University of Illinois Press, 1986.

people, and the true wealth for the colonies was the number and mix of people who came. Those who came represented a cosmopolitan and multicultural group, and the diggings were a melting pot of cultural complexity, ideas, ideals and political dissent. This group of people formed a generation that had a major impact on shaping Australia in the future. They were described by Geoffrey Serle as follows:

> *The Gold Generation dominated economic, social and public life for the remainder of the century.*[33]

News of the gold discovery quickly reached the United Kingdom. On 23 November 1852, three vessels arrived in the Thames, bringing between them seven tons of gold. One of the ships, the ***Eagle***, carried 150,000 ounces, which was the largest amount of the precious metal ever known to have been placed in one vessel at that time. The ***Eagle*** also made a record passage travelling from Melbourne to the Downs in 76 days, the shortest passage up to that period. A great sensation was caused by so much gold in one consignment, and it was carefully guarded on its way to the Bank of England. The arrival of the gold generated a huge amount of publicity and excitement in the United Kingdom. This marked the start of a mad rush to get to the colonies.

---

33   Serle, G. 'The Gold Generation'. Victorian Historical Journal, vol. 41, no. 1, 1970, p. 266.

> Then see us arrived at the shore,
> Rather sea-sick, but yet full of fun,
> As we think of our fortune in store,
> To which we are off with a run.

Disembarking and Off to the Diggings 1852
(State Library of Victoria)

It's interesting to note in 1852 'Australians officially became the richest people in the world, overtaking the British and the Dutch on the measure of GDP per person.'[34]

By the end of 1852, 88,000 people had left the United Kingdom and arrived in the colonies (nine out of 10 went directly to Victoria). More ships sailed to Melbourne than to any other port in the world. Another 63,000 arrived in 1853, followed by 83,000 in 1854.[35] During this period Australia received more free immigrants from the United Kingdom than it had received in the previous three decades of settlement.

It was not only men arriving and heading directly to the diggings. There were stories of women going to the diggings in search of a wealthy husband. This was captured in a humorous manner by artist John Leech:

---

34 Megalogenis, George. *Australia's Second Chance*. Penguin Hamish Hamilton, 2015, p. 73.
35 Emigration Commission, Thirty-Third General Report of the Emigration Commissioners, Appendix No. 1, pp 48–9.

Alarming Prospect: Single Ladies off to the Diggings 1853 by John Leech
(State Library of Victoria)

Unable to stop the flow of people to the goldfields La Trobe was concerned he would lose his public servants and so substantially increased their wages. Melbourne was losing a great number of workers to the goldfields and it was unable to deal with and accommodate the large numbers of immigrants arriving. La Trobe became convinced the gold rush was not a short-term event and he decided to embark on a massive program of infrastructure expenditure. His idea was to transform Melbourne into a modern metropolis. This resulted in significant expenditure on public works, including construction of roads, bridges, buildings, parklands, and transport and communication systems. The public works program created another economy operating in parallel with the gold mining that provided employment and opportunities for many who were not drawn to the goldfields. Many of those emigrants who paid their own fare to come to the colonies during this period were well educated, including many professionals seeking opportunities in Melbourne.

Charles Joseph La Trobe by John Botterill
(State Library of Victoria)

Not only were immigrants arriving in Victoria from the United Kingdom, America and Europe but there was also an enormous amount of inter-colonial movement. By late 1851, some 7000 gold seekers had arrived by sea from other colonies to join the rush to the diggings and hundreds more had tracked overland across the borders. In 1852 the inter-colonial flow intensified with ships bringing 14,000 from New South Wales, 19,000 from Tasmania, 15,000 from South Australia and Western Australia, and 1000 from New Zealand. Many thousands continued to come overland. South Australia and Tasmania lost half of their men.

As the vessels carrying emigrants to Victoria passed Cape Otway, the passengers would no doubt gaze at the coast, wondering what this new country would be like. On entering Port Phillip heads, a wide bay would unfold and then as Point Gellibrand came into sight the country would take shape, spirits would lift further, and the area would have the feel of a safe haven. However, at the time of the gold rush, it had indeed become a haven for vessels. The arriving emigrants would see hundreds of ships anchored in Hobsons Bay (later renamed Port

Phillip Bay), the crews having deserted and gone to the diggings. The captains of vessels were desperate to get their crews back and to proceed with the business of shipping. There were stories of crews being arrested for desertion and sentenced to a term of imprisonment. There was at least one case where a petition was made to the governor by the captain of a vessel to move the crew under guard to the vessel for immediate departure. La Trobe agreed, but the crew preferred to take their punishment and then go to the diggings.

There was a market area near Customs House where new arrivals could divest themselves of unwanted or non-essential items. Many of the new arrivals did this in order to acquire some cash or to lighten their load so they could proceed, carrying as little as possible to the diggings. Many went to Canvas Town—an area south of the River Yarra where new arrivals were permitted to pitch a tent until better accommodation could be acquired. The image below appeared in the *Supplement to the Illustrated Australian News* from a wood engraving using a sketch by S.T. Gill. Gill's sketch shows the considerable size of the Canvas Town, with a large number of vessels in the background lying idle in Port Phillip Bay.

Canvas Town in 1853 by S.T. Gill
(State Library of Victoria)

Once the full impact of the gold rush became apparent, La Trobe came under pressure from several sectors. Victoria had grown wealthy because of the successful pastoral industry; the direction for the colony had seemed assured, as it would grow as a wool-growing territory. However, the discovery of gold dramatically changed the future of Victoria. The nature of the problems for La Trobe caused by the gold rush changed as time elapsed. He now had to deal with new types of people with new skills, new ideas and philosophies, and who had new expectations. This was summarised nicely by Alan Gross writing about La Trobe when he compared pre–gold rush Victoria with post–gold rush Victoria:

> *…the mass which had followed the lure of gold, numerically greater and producing vaster wealth for export, but disfranchised, living life in the raw, and chafing under petty officialdom.* [36]

Many rural and urban employers in Victoria and the other colonies were left without labour. The pastoral lobby in Victoria was gravely concerned by the desertion of rural labourers and urged La Trobe to get as many assisted immigrants as possible to replace the agricultural workers that had deserted for the goldfields. This call for more assisted immigrants was echoed in the other colonies, as they had also lost many men to the Victorian goldfields. The effects of the gold rush were also being felt in the manufacturing towns of Yorkshire, which depended heavily on Australian wool. As a result, a committee was formed to petition the Prime Minister and Secretary of State to take steps urgently to supply the agricultural labour needed in the colonies.

The matter was raised in the House of Commons with a view to saving the next wool clip:

> *…a more immediate objective was to save the next wool clip… the Government was urged to send out in the course of June and July as many as 10,000 emigrants, and to spend …the whole of the emigration fund …amounting to …£331,000 …It became*

---
36 Gross, Alan. *Charles Joseph La Trobe.* Melbourne University Press, 1956, p. 113.

our duty to strain every nerve to mitigate …the catastrophe … supposed to be imminent.[37]

The colonies urged their immigration agents to act quickly to find suitable immigrants and hence pressure was exerted on the emigration commissioners to find immigrants and charter vessels to transport them to the colonies. The Emigration Commission was under increasing pressure from most of the colonies to find suitable immigrants and to despatch them as quickly as possible. The Commission was taken a little by surprise at the impact that the discovery of gold was having on the colonies and the numbers seeking to get to the goldfields. This is clear from comments made in their report for 1853:

> *We stated in our Report for last year that in the first instance the intelligence of the gold discoveries had had little effect in stimulating emigration to Australia, the spontaneous emigration of the last half of 1851 not having been greater than in the corresponding half of 1850. But in the first three months of 1852 the emigration increased to double that of the same period of 1851, and at the date of our Report (6th May 1852) it was going on very rapidly.*[38]

The report included a table that demonstrated the rapid growth in emigration to the colonies. In 1851 the number of people emigrating in ships chartered by the Commission was 21,532 and in 1852 the number had increased by over 66,000 to 87,882.

There was some consideration in the colonies about the types of immigrants the commissioners should concentrate on attracting as replacement labour. The colonies feared if single men came, they would immediately move to the diggings. Some felt older people may be reluctant to go to the goldfields and so might be a better prospect. Others felt young families with several children should be a priority

---

37 House of Commons Papers April 8 1853, Papers Relative to the Australian Colonies, Her Majesty's Stationary Office 1853, p. 138.

38 Report of The Colonial Land & Emigration Commission. British Parliamentary papers 1852–3, XI, (1647) pp. 65 CMSIED 212003–43.

as they would be less mobile and more likely to remain at the port of disembarkation.

The Emigration Commissioners, in responding to the requests, needed to find ways of getting as many people to the colonies as quickly as possible. They were faced with finding suitable emigrants and locating transport without delay. The effects of the gold rush made finding transport difficult. The vessels normally available to transport emigrants were largely engaged in taking paying passengers to seek their fortune on the goldfields. People of all classes were desperate to get there. There was chaos as these people besieged the shipping offices, begging for a place on any vessel going to the colonies. Charles Dickens described the crowds who gathered at the shipping offices as follows:

> *Legions of bankers' clerks, merchants' lads, embargo secretaries, and incipient cashiers; all going with the rush, and all possessing but faith and confused ideas of where they are going or what they are going to do; beg the hard-hearted shipbrokers to grant them the favour of a berth in their last-advertised, teak-built, poop-decked, copper-bottomed, double-fastened, fast-sailing, surgeon-carrying emigrant ship.*[39]

Puddling 1852 by S.T.Gill
(State Library of Victoria)

---

39 Searle, G.R. The Golden Age. Melbourne University Press, 1963, p. 44.

This enormous demand by gold seekers led to profit-taking by shipowners and agents, who preferred paying passengers to a ship load of emigrants. This shortage of shipping was further exacerbated because many vessels were taken off the Australian run, in order to transport British soldiers to the Crimean War. It was also clear many ships were deserted after arrival in Victoria, the crew having deserted and gone to the goldfields. This led the Emigration Commission to consider using some large North American–built vessels available out of Liverpool. These were vessels designed to transport cargo between North America and England, but the commissioners desperately needed transport for emigrants.

The demand by paying passengers had a significant impact on the charges vessel owners were asking the Emigration Commission to pay per head to transport emigrants to the colonies and it appears prices were also inflated because the shipowners feared crew members might desert on arrival and leave the ship stranded. These matters were raised in a letter dated 14 May 1852 from the Emigration Commission Secretary to the Victorian Colonial Secretary responding to the call for more immigrants. The last few paragraphs demonstrate the problems the Emigration Commission encountered in finding suitable vessels and at a reasonable cost:

> 11. You will observe from the accompanying table …that the contract price since the 1st November last has always been over twelve pounds per adult, and that since the 1st May, it has been but little under fourteen pounds; whereas in the first ten months of last year, the price for ships taken up previous to the receipt of intelligence of the gold discoveries was only in one case over eleven pounds, while in the rest it ranged from £9 9s 5d to £10 18s 0d per adult. This rise in price is principally due to fear entertained by the shipowners of the desertion of their crews on arrival and the consequent detention of the vessels, at a loss in time and money that it is impossible to calculate.

> *12. So strongly do the shipping interest feel this evil that many suggestions have been made to the Commissioners on this subject. Amongst others that a military or police force should be placed on board each ship while in port, to protect the desertion of the crew, or that the ship might be permitted to lie off at a distance from shore, and the emigrants be landed by means of a steamer to be provided at the expense of the owners. The Commission have submitted this last suggestion to the Secretary of State in case he should think fit to forward it for consideration of the Colonial Government.*
>
> *I am however to observe that unless the desertion of crews should be arrested, the rate of freight to Australia will doubtless continue to advance. Indeed, on some recent occasions, owing to this cause, and partly to the long prevalence of east winds, the Commission have received only one or two tenders in answer to their public advertisements for shipping, and had they not consented to take some of the very large vessels at Liverpool, they would have had to pay much higher rates than those shown in the enclosures.*[40]

Many of the older style emigration vessels had only been capable of transporting 250–350 emigrants and, while they were solid and reliable, they were not fast and were not available at a price the Emigration Commission was willing to pay. A potential solution emerged when some large North American–constructed vessels that could achieve a relatively fast passage to the colonies became available for charter. They could accommodate large numbers of passengers because they were double-deck vessels (i.e. they had two decks below the main deck for steerage passengers). These vessels had been designed and constructed to carry cargo, particularly timber, on the Atlantic route between North America and Britain. The large cargo area involving two decks could be converted easily for carriage of passengers—much

---

40 Letter from S. Walcott to W. Lonsdale 14 May 1852. Parliament of Victoria GP V 1852/53 Vol. 1 pp. 687–691.

like the older square-riggers were fitted for passengers on the outbound journey to the colonies and after arrival were gutted, ready for carrying cargo on the homebound journey. It was also possible that economies of scale could operate with large vessels because it may be possible to reduce the cost per immigrant by transporting larger numbers.

The Emigration Commissioners carefully checked the space available in the double-decker vessels to see that they complied with the requirements of statutory shipping regulations. In each case they had deck heights in excess of the six feet required in the current Passengers Act. It's interesting that a new Passenger Act was before Parliament that contained new requirements relating to provisions for emigrants and space requirements that would have imposed additional requirements on these vessels and any other vessel carrying emigrants. It also appeared to the commissioners, from available information, the larger the ship the lower the mortality rate on the run from Britain to North America.

On balance then, it seemed these vessels would be suitable for transporting large numbers of emigrants to the Australian colonies relatively quickly. Hence, the commissioners chartered six of these vessels in 1852. They were the **Bourneuf**, **Wanata**, **Marco Polo**, **Ticonderoga**, **Beejapore** and **Shackamaxon**. All six vessels could carry between 700 and 1000 passengers beneath the main deck.

The shipowners were required to sign a standard form of agreement (known as Form D No. 12) with the Emigration Commission. This was a lengthy document that included a table with a long list of medical items vessels needed to carry, including type and amount of each item for every 100 persons. It stipulated the medicines must be produced by the Apothecaries' Hall. Examples of items on the detailed list include: 1 oz. Acid Acetic, 1 oz. Acid Citric, 2 oz. Ferri Sulph., 6 yards of Flannel, 12 yards Calico, 2 male & 1 female syringes. The commissioners had established a set of requirements that had to be met by emigration vessels, including some that dealt with the health of emigrants. The health requirements particularly focussed on provision of medical supplies and the requirement to have a doctor (surgeon superintendent) on board. Hence each of these vessels should have been carrying the prescribed amount and type of medical supplies.

Following considerable pressure by the colonies to allow large families to emigrate, the commissioners also decided to relax their rules relating to the number and ages of children that could be transported on emigration vessels the Commission chartered.

And so, due to the intersection of a number of events in the middle of the nineteenth century, six very large vessels were chartered and sailed during 1852 for the colonies of New South Wales, Victoria and South Australia, with each carrying large numbers of emigrants (including many children) in very crowded conditions. The total number of emigrants to board the six vessels in 1852 was 4782 (crew and cabin passengers were additional to that number).

There is a story attached to the development and construction of each of these six ships, to their acquisition for the Australian run and the passage they made carrying an enormous number of emigrants to the colonies. What seemed like a good solution to the problem of needing to move many emigrants quickly to the colonies had unintended consequences.

Chapter 5

THE *BOURNEUF*

They built 'em in Annapolis, Windsor, River John
jest as able packets as you ever shipped upon
Yarmouth ships, Maitland ships, hookers from Maccan
The kind 'o craft that took the eye of any sailorman
Them fine old wind bags—them Nova Scotiamen.

Anon

THE ***BOURNEUF*** WAS built in Clare, Nova Scotia, in 1852. She had two decks below the main deck, was rigged as a three-mast ship and weighed 1496 tons.

In 1852 the ***Bourneuf*** was the first of the large North American–built vessels to be chartered by the Emigration Commissioners to transport emigrants to the colony of Victoria. She sailed from Liverpool on 26 May under Captain Robert Biddy and arrived at Geelong on 3 September 1852. There were 754 passengers on board. Many were Scots and there were also small numbers of English and Irish emigrants on board. Amongst the Scots were 20 that had been supported by the

Highland and Emigration Society, which played a major role in supporting Scots to emigrate.

The *Bourneuf* Docked at Birkenhead 1852
(Rex Nan Kivell Collection NK4182/89, National Library of Australia)

The arrival of the **Bourneuf** was announced in the *Argus* on Wednesday 8 September 1852 as follows:

> *The Bourneuf, emigrant ship, arrived off Point Henry yesterday, has been placed in quarantine. There have been eighty-three deaths on board since she left home, chiefly arising from scarlet fever and measles. The crew have all struck work, and I am told a boat is placed near her to watch that none of them desert. The vessel has upwards of 800 souls on board.*

When the ship reached Geelong, 88 passengers had died of measles, diarrhoea, scarlatina or marasmus (undernourishment) during the three months at sea (83 were children—almost half of the children on board). Most of the deaths were amongst the Scottish children under seven years old. When the ship arrived off Point Henry, she was placed in quarantine. A further 20 adults and children were still suffering from disease.

The deaths were the subject of an investigation by the Victorian health officer. His report includes the following:

> *Five women had died of consumption, puerperal fever, or been lost overboard. Of the 180 children under seven years of age who embarked, nearly half died of diarrhoea, measles, and other complaints ..*
>
> *Arrangements for hygiene were primitive or non-existent. The main deck leaked, so that the two migrant decks were usually damp. The water-closets were 'of inferior construction and leaky...'*
>
> *The upper immigrant deck had a 'disagreeable smell' while the lower deck was dark and 'difficult to ventilate'. There was insufficient hospital accommodation or spare bedding, so that infected mattresses had to be used again. The matron was almost useless 'owing to physical want of activity or energy', while Surgeon McKevit was accused by the passengers of being 'so grossly intoxicated that he could not attend to his duty'...*[41]

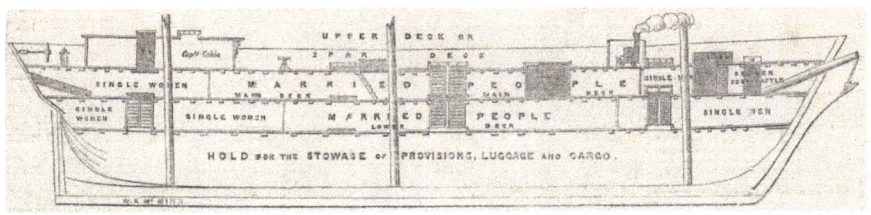

Below Decks Sketch of Ship *Bourneuf*
(Rex Nan Kivell Collection, NK4182/89, National Library of Australia)

This image of the ship's structure is taken from an article by W.K. McMinn published in the *Illustrated London News* on 10 July 1852 explaining the government-funded emigration system that

---

41 Strutt, C. E. to Colonial Secretary 22 September 1852.

provided assisted passage for those wanting to start a new life in the colonies. The drawing was provided to highlight the space available on an emigrant vessel and the physical separation between single men and single women, located safely away from each other at either end of the ship, with the families in between. The enquiry report also stated that, although the unmarried female passengers had been protected from the unmarried male passengers, they had not been able to prevent contact and fraternisation with the crew. The passengers' galley entered directly into the crew's galley. When the ship docked at Geelong, the seamen rioted and police had to be called to control them and ensure they didn't desert ship. They clearly had ideas of joining the gold rush.

Yarra Street Pier Geelong by T.W. Cameron
(State Library of Victoria)

The Immigration Board of Geelong also investigated the deaths and sickness on board the ***Bourneuf*** and concluded in its report of 22 September 1852:

> ...Should it, nevertheless, be deemed expedient to charter a vessel similar to the "Bourneuf" the Board would suggest, that the number of immigrants embarked should be diminished; that the space thus gained should be rendered available for the school; that the appointments of schoolmaster and matron should be left to the Surgeon-Superintendent; that ventilators should be fitted with wire netting, to prevent unnecessary communication or conversation between the crew and the single females. The hospital accommodation for women and children should be increased.
>
> C.E. Strutt, Assistant Emigration Agent,
>
> W.H. Baylie, Deputy Surgeon,
>
> Charles Friend, Harbour Master.[42]

The Board also commented in its report that a major cause of death among the children was:

> ...the insurmountable prejudice of the Scotch and Irish parents against administering any medicines to their children, and their neglect of medical measures proposed.

Many of the Scottish and Irish passengers were from small rural communities, were accustomed to traditional and folk remedies and were suspicious of urban medicines and practices. It also seems some emigrants only spoke Gaelic, which created further problem for the surgeon superintendent (who was reported to be incompetent).

There had been trouble with some of the crew refusing to do their duty during the passage and with one crew member being placed in irons for striking the captain. According to a police report in the *Argus* on 16 September 1862, six men were charged as a result of a statement by the captain. These men were remanded in custody pending receipt

---

42 Papers Relative to Emigration to the Australian Colonies. Report of the Immigration Board at Geelong, upon the Immigrant Ship 'Bourneuf', 22 September 1852, Encl. 4 in No. 22.

of further evidence. Despite efforts to ensure the crew remained on board soon after arrival at that port, most of her 58 crew deserted and headed to the goldfields. The Bourneuf was forced to sit in Geelong for several months but eventually got under way on 7 May 1853 with the assistance of a pilot at a cost of £15 and was bound for Bombay. She made her way up the east coast of Australia and was wrecked on the Great Detached Reef as she was about to enter the Torres Strait. Seven lives were lost.

The *Bourneuf* was the first of the large North American–built vessels to arrive in Australia carrying emigrants. The news of the tragic loss of life on this voyage soon found its way back to the home country and to the Emigration Commission. The Commission was appalled by the news and decided not to use double-decker vessels in the future. When it saw that the majority of deaths were among the children it also announced it would reintroduce the policy whereby no family with more than two children under seven years or three children under 10 years would be accepted for emigration. However, by the time the Commission had received news of the *Bourneuf* the other five large vessels that it had engaged were under way carrying large numbers of emigrants. It's interesting that the statement by the Commission not to use double-deck vessels again was later revisited, possibly as a result of deciding their use may be appropriate under a new set of conditions, including reducing the number of passengers close to what would have been carried on single-deck vessels; reducing the number of children; and ensuring the surgeon superintendent was competent, experienced and fully aware of his responsibilities.

There were also new requirements introduced as a result of the new Passengers Act[43], which was passed by Parliament on 30 June 1852 and came into effect on 1 October. However, these new requirements were too late to apply to the large vessels already chartered by the

---

43 An 'Act to amend and consolidate the laws relating to the Carriage of Passengers by Sea', but which, by Clause 2, can be cited under the abbreviated title of 'The Passengers Act, 1852'.

Commission. The principal alterations that it introduced were the extension of its provisions to Australian and American emigration; the change in the size of berths and the separation of single men from the other passengers; the enforcement of a scale of hospital accommodation and privies; the regulation of the stowage of heavy cargo; the assimilation in quality of the provisions of the emigrants and crew; the removal and marking of bad provisions; the issue of cooked provisions instead of uncooked; the employment of passenger stewards, of interpreters, and of medical men in specified cases; and the recovery from the owner, charterer or master of the expense of assisting shipwrecked emigrants.

Chapter 6

THE *WANATA*

> *The creatures of a passing race,*
> *The dark spruce forests made them strong,*
> *The sea's lore gave them magic grace,*
> *The great winds taught them song.*
>
> *Ships of Saint John*, Bliss Carman

THE *WANATA* WAS constructed in 1851 in Oromocto, New Brunswick, using hackmatack, elm, birch and pitch pine. She was classified as a vessel with three decks (i.e. the main deck and two further decks below), weighing 1443 tons and rigged as a three-mast ship.

The *Wanata,* like many vessels constructed in New Brunswick, was sold to a Liverpool shipowner (Barton & Co.). She was registered in Liverpool in 1852 and subsequently sheathed in copper in readiness for the Australian run. It's likely her name came from North American Indians; Wanata was a chief of one of the Dakota tribes.

A Typical New Brunswick Ship Yard

New Brunswick Harbour

The ***Wanata*** was the second of the large North American–built vessels to be chartered by the Emigration Commissioners in 1852 to transport emigrants to Melbourne. As with the ***Bourneuf***, the decision to use the ***Wanata*** was largely made because of her size and therefore ability to accommodate a large number of passengers in a double-deck configuration.

She sailed from Liverpool on Thursday 10 June 1852, carrying 820 passengers. The master for the voyage was Captain J. Lee and the surgeon superintendent was William Thomson, assisted by a second doctor (Dobbin). Although there were two decks for steerage-class passengers, she was still badly overcrowded with such a large number of passengers.

As a double-decked vessel, the ***Wanata*** was not only overcrowded, but like the ***Bourneuf***, it was inadequately ventilated, particularly in the second deck. This was a common problem with the two-decked vessels. As with other overcrowded vessels, this made the ship susceptible to the spread of contagious illness and disease. It wasn't long into the voyage when signs of typhus fever and whooping cough emerged. These diseases were the cause of death of 39 passengers during the voyage.

On arrival on 17 September 1852, 97 days after departing, she sailed into Hobsons Bay, flying the yellow flag. She anchored off Gelibrand Point (near Williamstown), with 796 government emigrants aboard. She had left Liverpool with 820 emigrants. Of the 39 deaths, 33 were children. The discrepancy in the total number that arrived is most probably explained by births during the voyage. The six adult deaths had the following causes recorded: one from apoplexy, one from consumption and four from fever (probably typhus fever).

Dr Hunt, the health officer of the port, visited the ship and ordered her to quarantine offshore between Brighton and St Kilda. The quarantine station at Portsea was established approximately one month later in November. The schooner, ***Apollo***, was stationed nearby as a guard ship to prevent passengers from escaping from the ***Wanata*** until the authorities lifted the quarantine restrictions. It was proposed to release the ship from quarantine after a week had passed, but on 23 September, a new case of fever was reported.

All the sick passengers were then transferred to the schooner, **Fanny,** which lay nearby, and the **Fanny** was then also placed in quarantine. There were five more deaths among the sick passengers. On 4 October, the **Wanata** was allowed to leave the quarantine area and join the other ships in the bay, and arrangements were made for the migrants to disembark. The Port Health Officer stated in his annual report for 1853:

> *The Wanata. – This ship reported on her arrival that eighteen cases of typhus fever had occurred on the voyage, twenty of pertussis, and a few of measles, and that typhus fever then existed. The sick were transhipped into the Fanny, a vessel of 950 tons, hired for the purpose of an hospital ship, where three adults died of fever. She received pratique on the 4th October.*[44]

Passengers Arriving in Melbourne After Quarantine
(Australasian Sketcher, State Library of Victoria)

---

44 Annual Report of Health Officer, Thomas Hunt, 1 May 1852 to 30 June 1853, p. 7. Parliament of Victoria GP V 1853/54 no. A42.

There was much criticism in the newspapers regarding the overcrowding permitted on the **Wanata**. The Immigration Board conducted an enquiry into the **Wanata** and reported in 1852. The report contained the following comments:

> 2. *The Health Officer upon visiting the ship, deemed it necessary to place her in quarantine, many deaths having occurred during the voyage, and several cases of sickness and fever of a typhoid nature still remaining on board.*
>
> 6. *The fittings of this vessel were in many respects very imperfect, as had been frequently found to be the case in other ships despatched from the same port. The water closets, more especially, appear to have been a source of constant annoyance, and even to have threatened serious consequences, from the difficulty of obtaining proper cleanliness and ventilation.*
>
> 7. *… The Board are of the opinion, that it is manifestly unadvisable that two-decked ships should be employed in the conveyance of so large a number of passengers.*
>
> *… The Surgeon superintendent distinctly traces the origin of fatal illness in many instances…. to the exposure of a large number of the immigrants to a whole night's drenching rain, on the steamer from Glasgow to Liverpool.*
>
> 14. *In conclusion, the Board cannot avoid remarking upon the inexpediency of embarking so large a number of souls in one ship. The danger to the general health incurred thereby, and the difficulty of thorough ventilation being, in their opinion, irresistible arguments against the continuance of the system.*
>
> *Edward Grimes, Chairman.*[45]

---

45 Papers Relative to Emigration to the Australian Colonies. Report of the Immigration Board Melbourne upon the 'Wanata', Encl. 3 in No. 22, Immigration Office, Melbourne October 21 1852.

The officials in Victoria were clearly of the view the double-deck arrangements on the *Wanata* were a key reason for the 39 deaths during the voyage (including 30 children) and the further five deaths during quarantine. They were of the view double-deck vessels had no place in the future transportation of emigrants to Victoria.

Despite the criticism that accompanied the arrival of the *Wanata* in 1852, she made a second voyage to Melbourne the next year, departing not from Liverpool but from Southampton on 25 October 1853. The surgeon superintendent was John Farmer. The passengers were listed as assisted immigrants in the Victorian Immigration Agents Report for 1854 and the contract price per statute adult was recorded as £16 19s 9d. After 89 days at sea, she berthed on 22 January 1854 with 342 souls onboard (including 68 children—almost 20 per cent of the total).

It would appear she was engaged to operate as a single-deck vessel, carrying less than half the number of passengers she carried on the first passage to Victoria. This voyage resulted in a very different health outcome to that experienced in 1852: while there were 13 deaths (eight adults and five children—no infants) on the passage to Melbourne, this represented a significant improvement to that of its first voyage to the colony. The crew was described as being 'in a state of mutiny' on arrival and some deserted in a pilot's boat prior to the ship berthing on 21 January. Clearly some crew members were very keen to remain in the colony, no doubt influenced by the stories of gold discoveries.

In 1860 the *Wanata* was purchased by the Black Ball Line and remained part of that line until the end of her life.

The *Wanata* made a third voyage to the colonies, this time to Queensland in 1862 under the command of Captain Murphy. She departed London on the 2 November 1862, sailed to Ireland and then departed Queenstown on the 12 November 1862. The voyage ended on 17 February 1863. On Friday 13 February the *Everton* and the

Wanata were anchored off the northern end of Moreton Island with pilots on board waiting for favourable conditions to enable them to cross the bay to the usual anchorage at the bar. The emigrants on both vessels were no doubt celebrating a safe arrival and looking forward to disembarking in Brisbane. What they were not aware of was an approaching cyclone and that the most dangerous part of the voyage was yet to come. At noon a cyclonic gale struck both vessels and they were only saved by the skill of the pilots. Steam tugs were not available and so both vessels had to slip anchors and head out to sea and hope for a favourable opportunity to get into port. The *Brisbane Courier* on 16 February reported:

> *The captain of the Wanata declared it to be the worst part of the voyage and all who witnessed the gale unite in stating that it was the worst they had experienced for many years past.*

For this voyage the number was again increased, with 638 passengers on board, but it was significantly less than the 820 transported on the first voyage to the colonies. The number was possibly increased because the Emigration Commission was not involved in that voyage. There were seven deaths on the voyage. The ship's surgeon superintendent was Dr Burke. The arrival was described in the *Courier* on Friday 20 February 1863 as follows:

THE WANATA.

> *The whole of the passengers by this vessel were brought up to Brisbane yesterday in the steamers Brisbane and Samson. In all, they number 636 individuals, about one-half of whom come out under the auspices of the Queensland Immigration Society. They seem a very respectable class of people and are all in excellent health. Only seven deaths occurred during the passage, all of which – with the single exception of a young man who was ill with consumption before he embarked were infants. But as a sort of counterbalance to this mortality, there were five births. This vessel is remarkable*

for having brought the largest number of immigrants ever landed on our shores from one ship, and also, when everything is taken into consideration, for the small number of casualties.

The Queensland Government was keen to attract immigrants to the relatively new colony and had sent emigration agents to Britain and Germany to point out the advantages offered by the new colony, such as a healthy and mild climate, as against the more rigorous climate in Canada and New Zealand. Canada and New Zealand, as well as the other Australian colonies, were also competing vigorously for settlers and these two countries were offering grants of land on very liberal terms.

The Queensland Government, however, devised a scheme by offering all full-paying passengers an £18 land order, which could be used in part payment for any land taken up on arrival in the colony and, after a continuous residence of two years in Queensland, another land order for £12 was given. Assisted passengers (i.e. those who paid only half the usual fee of £17 steerage class), were also to receive a land order of £12 at the end of two years' residence. This scheme proved very attractive to many, for it appeared passengers would receive a land order worth £18 on landing, because they had paid £17 passage money. Those in England or Queensland who wished to pay the passages of servants, family or friends could also receive the £18. It was considered by the emigrants to be equivalent to obtaining a free passage and for the Queensland Government of getting a superior class of immigrant. This scheme was provided for under the Alienation of Crown Land Act of 1860 and it authorised the governor with the advice of the Executive Council to make the payments.

The Roman Catholic Bishop of Queensland, James Quinn, was actively involved in attracting and supporting emigrants from Ireland. He arrived in the colony in the **Donald Mackay** on 10 December 1860. On his voyage he conceived the notion of grand scale emigration to his new diocese. He felt there were people in Ireland that needed to emigrate, and if the Queensland colony was prepared to pay Land Orders to the eventual value of £30 to attract immigrants from Europe, then it was a simple matter of logistics. In order to make large-scale immigration work, he needed to set up machinery to make it happen as the Queensland Government wasn't going to organise it for him. To do this, he set up the Queensland Immigration Society and created a fund by seeking donations locally and in Ireland. The idea was to assist Irish immigrants by paying the passage or subsidising it and then to claim the land order payment on arrival, which would refinance the fund and pay the passage of the next group. The notice from the *Courier* on the previous page shows a number of the Irish emigrants on the **Wanata** had travelled under sponsorship of the Queensland Immigration Society.

One of the passengers recorded the passage as follows:

> *The Wanata left London November 2, Queenstown November 12, crossed the Line December 8, was in the longitude of the Cape in January 2, and made the run from thence to Tasmania in 28 days. Here she encountered adverse winds, which greatly impeded her course, but up to this period favourable winds and smooth seas were the characteristics of everyday. Land was sighted February 11, and the anchor was dropped off the Light-house on Thursday, February 12, thus completing the voyage from Queenstown in 91 days. The very large number of passengers conveyed by her have arrived in the most satisfactory state of health, even the temporary ailings during the voyage being much below the average, and the casualties very few, and, with one exception, all of these were young and weakly children. The only adult casualty was that of a young man who was consumptive when he embarked, and whose life had altogether been despaired of.*[46]

---

46 Courier, 20 February 1863, p. 2.

It appears that captain and doctor were both highly regarded by the passengers and the passage was reported to have been well organised, and discipline and order were maintained. Some two-thirds of the passengers had embarked at Queenstown and they were mostly of a Roman Catholic faith. They were accompanied by a Roman Catholic chaplain, Rev. J. J. Curley, who assisted with supporting passengers and maintaining order, and a Presbyterian minister from Ireland, Rev. John Wilson, who also assisted in supporting the passengers. Groups were formed during the passage, briefed and given responsibilities directed at maintaining the health, wellbeing and happiness of the passengers. It's possible that having fewer passengers, combined with the organisation and support arrangements on this passage by the **Wanata**, were responsible for the small number of deaths compared to the previous passages. Another factor is she departed from London and not Liverpool.

A fourth passage was made to the colonies in 1864. This time the **Wanata** carried passengers to Sydney, arriving in September. It seems the passengers on this voyage were sponsored or bounty emigrants. The *Sydney Morning Herald* carried the following notice on 5th September 1864:

> IMMIGRANTS PER WANATA – *Notice is hereby given that the undermentioned persons, for whom passages have been provided in this colony, in pursuance of deposits made in this office, under the Assisted Immigration Regulations, have arrived in the ship Wanata, and that they will be prepared to join their friends-the SINGLE FEMALES from the Depot, Hyde Park, and the MARRIED PEOPLE and SINGLE MEN from on board the vessel, as soon as released from Quarantine, of which due notice will be given. (the report concluded with a list of passengers and the names of the depositors)*

This was the **Wanata's** last passage to the Australian colonies.

The *Wanata* sank on 6 February 1866 after colliding with the *Queen of Beauty* in the Bay of Biscay. The *Queen of Beauty* had departed London on 2 January, bound for Melbourne. On 6 February, towards midnight in a very heavy sea and a thick haze, a vessel was reported on the lee bow. Although action was taken immediately to avoid collision, the *Queen of Beauty* struck the *Wanata* on the port side Attempts were made by the ship's carpenter to patch the hole, but due to the heavy seas they were not successful. The *Wanata* had left Liverpool with 183 passengers and cargo, including iron and coal under Captain Todd. The passengers were transferred to the *Queen of Beauty* and subsequently taken to Plymouth before being taken back to Liverpool. After the passengers and crew had abandoned the *Wanata,* she caught fire. By this stage in her life of some 15 years she had started to leak badly, particularly on a starboard tack.

Chapter 7

THE *MARCO POLO*

To the Black Ball Line she soon was sold
Australia bound in search of gold......
For thirty-two years she ran the tide
On Cavendish shoal she finally died
But dreams are much too hard to kill
The Marco Polo's living still.[47]

THERE WERE SEVERAL Canadian shipbuilding centres that were active during the nineteenth century. One such centre was Saint John, New Brunswick. Strategically located where the Saint John River flows into the Bay of Fundy, Saint John was bound on its landward side by many active shipyards. There were many fine shipwrights working in New Brunswick during the nineteenth century. One of those was James Smith, who had been born in Northern Ireland.

Between 1836 and 1842, Smith and his crew, built ships for several owners. After 1842 Smith became both builder and owner of all the ships constructed by his crews. By 1850 the Smith shipyard had built

---

47   Taken from a folk opera about the *Marco Polo* composed by Canadian Jim Stewart.

18 large ships, mainly for the purpose of carrying cargo. Smith kept abreast of developments in ship design, including the faster clipper ships, which were exciting because of their speed and beauty. Smith decided his next ship would be a large square-rigged vessel, which would incorporate clipper characteristics, including an ability to sail at high speeds even in rough weather. His aim was to build a ship that would be attractive and sell quickly in the Liverpool market.

James Smith ca. 1851 (Ship *Marco Polo* in the background)
(New Brunswick Museum – Musée du Nouveau-Brunswick, www.nbm-mnb.ca, 1945.762)

Construction of the ship, which Smith called **Marco Polo** (after the Venetian explorer), commenced in the autumn of 1850 at Marsh Creek, New Brunswick. A key step in the construction was the development of a half model of the vessel. At this time plans were rarely used in shipbuilding, but it was common practice to construct a model of half of the ship from bow to stern along its midline (the entire hull was not needed as each half was the same). The half model of the **Marco Polo** has survived and can be seen in the Mariner's Museum, Newport News, Virginia.

Martin Hollenberg commented that the model:

> ... held together by dowels, shows a vessel with sharp ends and a full rounded hull amidships. Definitely not pretty to look at, the model reveals a ship that, for its time, would have had a huge carrying capacity for lumber or people.[48]

The **Marco Polo** was completed in April 1851 after a construction period of about 18 months. She weighed 1625 tons, with a keel of 185 feet long, a beam amidships of 35 feet and a depth of its hold of 29 feet. It had three decks, eight feet apart and three masts square rigged. The figurehead was a life-size carving of Marco Polo. On its stern there were further carvings of Marco Polo and an elephant and a star. The launch wasn't without problems, as reported in the *New Brunswick Courier* 19 April 1851:

> *A large and elegant vessel called the MARCO POLO was launched on Thursday morning last from the building yard of Mr. James Smith at Courtenay Bay. He is also the owner. She has three complete decks, measures 1625 tons, and her length aloft is upwards of 184 feet. We presume that although not quite the largest that has been built in the Province this splendid ship is probably the longest that has been built in the Province. She is named after the celebrated Venetian traveller who discovered the coast of Malabar.*
>
> *We regret to learn that after this fine vessel had got clear of her ways in launching, she touched the bank of the creek and the wind blowing fresh at the time, went over on her beam ends, in consequence of which, some of the persons on board were hurt. One boy saved himself by jumping overboard and swimming ashore. The vessel, we understand, was not injured.*

---

48 Hollenberg Martin J. Marco Polo, the Story of the Fastest Clipper. Nimbus Publishing 2006, p. 18.

Carvings on Stern of *Marco Polo*
Marco Polo's Head (Left)
Marco Polo Reclining - Eastern Dress (Right)
(Wikimedia)

Frederick Wallace described the **Marco Polo** as follows:

The Marco Polo was not a clipper in the true sense of the term, but she was of sharper model under water than the usual craft built at Saint John and was regarded as a distinct departure from the common run of ships before her. Above the water, she was lofty and somewhat box-like – a great roomy, heavily-timbered vessel designed to pack a huge cargo and yet sail well. The true clipper was too sharp to carry much cargo, but in Marco Polo James Smith combined carrying capacity with an under-water body of sharp entrance and clean run – the true hollow bows of the clipper model being embodied – but amidships she had a bilge of the cargo-carrier.[49]

Smith sailed the **Marco Polo** to Liverpool, where he sold it to a marine dealer and shipbroker, Paddy McGee. Because the **Marco Polo** took some time to sell, no more vessels of that size were built at Saint John until 1855. McGee then sold **Marco Polo** to James Baines and his

---

49 Wallace, Frederick. Wooden Ships and Iron Men. Hodder and Stoughton, 1924, p.126.

associates and she became part of the Black Ball Line of vessels. She was then dry docked for an extensive refit to transform her from a timber carrier into a passenger liner. At the same time iron fittings were replaced with copper ones and the hull was completely covered with sheets of copper.

Marco Polo by John Goodchild
(State Library of Western Australia)

The ***Marco Polo*** was now ready to take her place as an emigrant vessel on the Australian run. In June 1852 the Emigration Commissioners chartered the steerage accommodation on the ***Marco Polo*** and the charter agreement was for some 750 emigrants to be accommodated and transported to Melbourne. This suited Baines as it ensured financial success for this first passage to the colonies. It was also fortuitous for the Emigration Commissioners that the ***Marco Polo*** was newly refitted for passengers and was available given the shortage of vessels due to the gold rush and for the Black Ball Line, as they had an assured 'cargo'.

Even for a very large vessel like the ***Marco Polo***, with 750 emigrants the conditions on board would be crowded. The Emigration Commissioners were keen to keep the emigrants moving toward their destination and, as with the ***Bourneuf*** and ***Wanata,*** the ***Marco Polo***'s size and capacity appeared to be a good solution to the shortage of vessel space.

The emigrants came mainly from Scotland and included single men and women, married couples and 327 children and infants. In addition to the 750 emigrants, there were also approximately 138 cabin- and intermediate-class passengers and a crew of 30 regular seamen and 30 others who were working to earn a passage to the goldfields. The Black Ball Line had also engaged a surgeon superintendent (D. B. North) and a second doctor for the passage to Melbourne. Hence, for the maiden passage to Melbourne, the ***Marco Polo*** carried almost 950 passengers and crew.

The emigrants were required to assemble in Liverpool prior to boarding the ***Marco Polo***. Even though the steerage passengers had their passage paid for by the Emigration Commissioners, they had to visit the Black Ball Line Office at 6 Cook Street, close to the Mersey River to receive their 'ticket' and have their luggage registered and labelled for eventual placement in the ship's hold. The ticket was like a contract with the Black Ball Line, which listed the name of the ship, the class of accommodation and meals, and contained an undertaking by the line to provide the transport to the specified destination. Most of the emigrants embarking in Liverpool would have arrived there before the ship departed and may have required cheap lodgings of the sort available in the overcrowded, pest-ridden and dirty lodging houses. Some fell victim to one or more of the many contagious diseases endemic in Liverpool at that time. Others unknowingly incubated infectious diseases and carried them onto ships like the ***Marco Polo.***

A few days before boarding the ship, the emigrants were able to move into the emigrant depot at Birkenhead, which had been opened in 1852. The depot was located across the Mersey from Liverpool and the Black Ball Line office. The emigrants were crowded together at the Birkenhead depot just like they would be on board the *Marco Polo*. Because the Birkenhead depot could only accommodate 400 people at a time, the emigrants would have been processed in at least two groups, with those not in the first group being exposed to the local community for an additional four days (the time usually taken to process emigrants prior to embarkation).

The steerage passengers were taken on board first and underwent a health inspection carried out by the two ships' surgeons, supervised by Captain Charles Schomberg and his team from the emigration office. The inspection was quick and superficial. The main purpose was to detect any active infectious diseases, but it was not possible to detect any potential illness during the incubation period.

In the steerage-class areas of the ship the single males were accommodated forward, the single females aft and the families amidships. There were partitions dividing the three groups. No space was wasted in the steerage compartments on the two decks below the main deck. The berths were about six feet square and four to six people were accommodated in each one. Double bunks, placed one on top of the other, were commonly used with children crowded below. There was virtually no privacy and little room between the bunks. There were separate toilets for men and women and long tables and benches were placed in the centre of the room.

The *Marco Polo* departed for Melbourne on 4 July 1852 with much fanfare, including the flying of flags around the port, a band playing rousing music and the firing of the ship's cannon. Once the ship reached open water in the Irish Sea, the passengers would have encountered the pitching and rolling of the *Marco Polo* for the first time. At that point many would have experienced seasickness. For some it would last for days and for others it would reoccur many times during the passage. Now that the vessel was at sea, the classes of passengers were largely kept separate. However, infectious diseases were a threat to all classes of passengers as they could jump from steerage to intermediate to cabin class. The surgeons on the ship made daily inspections and emphasised cleanliness, frequent washing and good ventilation. However, this was not always successful in stopping the spread of disease, particularly as many of the passengers were not familiar with or convinced of the usefulness of such practices.

Marco Polo **1859 by Thomas Robertson.**
(State Library of Victoria)

The Black Ball Line appointed the young James Nicol Forbes as the captain of the **Marco Polo** for her maiden voyage to the colonies. He had previously worked for the line as master of the **Maria** and then the **Cleopatra**, both on the Australia run. Forbes quickly developed a reputation as a bold, aggressive captain and gained the nickname: 'Bully' Forbes. He was apparently known for his hair-trigger temper, his boastfulness and his abusive attitude to his crew and even his passengers. He was said to have told his passengers at the start of his second voyage on the ***Marco Polo***:

> Ladies and Gentlemen, last trip I astounded the world with the sailing of this ship. This trip, I intend to astonish God Almighty!

Having been given the captaincy of this large new vessel, Forbes was determined to make a name for himself and create a record by sailing to the colonies and back to Liverpool in a record time. He wanted to depart as quickly as possible, which resulted in inadequate supplies being loaded, and stores and passenger trunks not being stowed correctly. Forbes was prepared to push both the ship and the crew to their limits to achieve his goal. While he was confident and brash, he was also a highly trained seaman. Forbes knew of the work of John Towson (described in Chapter 1) and was impressed with the new great circle route to the colonies and back to England. Using this route and pushing the crew and vessel, Forbes set a new record for a voyage around the world. To the amazement of many, the voyage to Melbourne and back to Liverpool was made in five months and 21 days. As a reward for his success, Forbes was given command of the ***Marco Polo*** for a second passage in 1853.

The *Illustrated London News* on 19 February 1853, in a long article, made the following remarks about the fast passage of the ***Marco Polo***:

> ...a noble British ship – the Marco Polo – had already sailed from the Mersey and was destined to achieve a triumph over both sailing-vessels and steamers greater than had ever before been considered possible by nautical men. The Marco Polo sailed from Liverpool, with a complement of passengers, on 4th of July, for Port Phillip, and made the voyage out in the unprecedentedly short space of sixty-eight days! And the passage home in seventy-four days! Allowing for twenty-eight days spent unloading and loading at Port Phillip, only five months and twenty-eight days elapsed from her leaving and regaining the shores of Great Britain.

While Bully Forbes was urging his ship on, driving this new clipper through the seas under full sail, between the decks the emigrants and their children were dying at the rate of nearly one every day. Because Forbes' objective was to arrive in the shortest possible time, there was no heaving to for sea burials. The rough pine coffins used on the ***Marco Polo*** were simply slid overboard, where they bobbed up and down in the ship's wake and were soon lost from sight. Some families left Liverpool with several children and arrived in Melbourne with none. The ship was grossly overcrowded, carrying more passengers than it was licensed to carry. Every available space was used to accommodate emigrants. The after part of the upper deck—only five feet high and not intended to accommodate passengers—was at the last minute fitted up for extra emigrants. As a result, the galleys were too small to cook for the number on board, the ventilators couldn't be opened in big seas and the ship's matron was ineffective. Many of the emigrants were unprepared for sailing in the Great Southern Ocean and were affected by the extreme cold, including a vicious storm with flurries of snow. These conditions aggravated the measles, pneumonia, diarrhoea, whooping cough and catarrh, which swept through the ***Marco Polo.***

There were 52 deaths during the voyage. A comment was made that as most emigrants were hardy Scottish highlanders and Skye islanders, this probably prevented an even higher mortality. While this comment may be true for adults, the children and infants were much more susceptible to illness and infectious diseases, especially measles. Children were often weakened by malnutrition and there were times during the voyage when parents were also ill or weak from seasickness and unable to care for their children. The surgeons would have quickly recognised the blotchy rash that came with measles accompanied by a high fever. However, there was little they could do for the victim. While they were aware measles was highly contagious, it was almost impossible for them to isolate those who were infected because of the extreme crowding on the ship. During the 1852 passage, of the 327 children onboard, 52 died in a measles epidemic. This represented 15.9 per cent of the children, which is much higher than the proportion that died from measles on land at that time. For example, the death rate from measles in Glasgow in the middle of the nineteenth century was only about 0.1 per cent.

The passengers and crew would have been relieved when they saw Cape Otway for the first time. They then had only 60 nautical miles to the entrance of Port Phillip Bay. It was Sunday, 19 September when the **Marco Polo** reached her anchorage in Hobsons Bay, west of the entrance to the Yarra Yarra River. The captain was surprised to see as many as 50 large ships lying idle as he'd expected to see much activity involving crew loading or unloading cargo. He soon discovered the reason for the idle ships was that crew had deserted and rushed to the goldfields. This made him think his crew might do likewise and thus prevent him from setting the record for a round trip Liverpool to Liverpool and so he devised a plan to have his crew locked up for insubordination. This was reported some time later in the *Australian and New Zealand Gazette* on 1 January 1853:

> *On arrival of the Marco Polo, such was the excitement on account of her rapid passage, that the people threw small nuggets of gold aboard among the crew. The crew having become unruly, Captain Forbes had the whole of them imprisoned until his departure and was thus able to get off again without loss of time. Many ships are laid up in Melbourne, for want of hands, which cannot be obtained at any price. One ship had advertised for men at the rate of 30 shillings per month, but no application was made.*

Although this report may have embellished the story of what happened, Forbes' plot worked and his men were released on payment by Forbes of their fine and they were available for the return passage. The ship was ready to depart only three weeks after arriving.

***Marco Polo* by J Johnson**
(State Library of Victoria)

Because of the high death rate on the passage from Liverpool, the Victorian Immigration Board conducted an investigation and presented its report on 2 October 1852. The report contained the following comments:

> *3. The Board at the same time remark: – 1st. That the number of statute adults which the ship was chartered to carry was only 701, while the number embarked was 749 ½...*
>
> *2nd. From the Surgeons Journal it appears that the ship was despatched with undue haste from Liverpool, the decks are reported to have been lumbered with luggage...*
>
> *3rd. The galley was decidedly too small and not arranged with much judgement... the skylights and ventilators were carelessly made.*

10. The master selected the great circle course between the longitude of the Cape and the port. The Board doubt the propriety of this choice, unless the immigrants are previously warned of the cold weather which they will experience, and the proper precautions for their health are taken. In the present case, the extreme cold appears by the Surgeon's Journal to have aggravated the diseases on board, and to have probably increased the extent of mortality.

11. In conclusion, the Board desire to express their decided objection (in which they believe that the mass of their fellow colonists join) to the selection of large vessels carrying passengers on two decks, for the conveyance at the public expense of emigrants to this colony.

Hugh C. E. Childers, Chairman[50]

The ***Marco Polo***'s arrival in September 1852 was the third North American–built vessel to arrive in Hobsons Bay and all three had experienced high death rates of emigrants on the passage from Liverpool to Victoria. The Immigration Board had conducted an enquiry into each of the three vessels and made similar comments about overcrowding and the undesirability of using large vessels with two decks to transport emigrants to the colony of Victoria. However, by the beginning of October 1852 three more double-deck vessels were already on their way to the colonies of Victoria, New South Wales and South Australia.

Despite the findings of the Immigration Board on the ***Marco Polo***, she was soon on her second passage to Melbourne. On that voyage she also departed from Liverpool, arriving in Melbourne on 30 May 1853 and quickly departing for Liverpool on 7 June. She was again captained by Forbes and he was determined to do the second return trip back to Liverpool in a quicker time. As in the first voyage, this meant much discomfort to the passengers as the captain took the vessel into

---

50 Papers Relative to Emigration to the Australian Colonies. Report of the Immigration Board upon the ship 'Marco Polo' encl. 2 in No. 22, Immigration Office Melbourne, October 2 1852.

the Great Southern Ocean and pushed the vessel and crew. This is illustrated in the following remarks taken from the diary of passenger Edwin Bird:

> ...the Captain says that we are a full 2 days in advance of his last voyage...
>
> ...every lady on board was sea sick and a great deal of the men. Going 12 nots (sic) an hour...
>
> ...the Captain is on deck almost night and day watching the sails and helm and there's no doubt we shall make a quick passage....
>
> ...gale and heavy seas which made us roll awful breaking plates dishes upsetting forms giving young ladies black eyes by being thrown from their bunks, upsetting soup, breaking legs ...passengers thrown from one end of the deck to the other...
>
> ...has been very cold snow rain and sleet... [51]

The documents and diaries also show Captain Forbes dealt quickly and severely with any misbehaviour by the crew and passengers. An example of this is included in the 1853 diary of passenger William Culshaw Greenhalgh:

> Friday 22nd April. A Sale by Auction from 10 until 1 PM the articled did not sell so well some went below cost price, almost calm making little or no progress. A man put in Irons for insulting the first Mate & being drunk was put in Irons for several days fed upon bread & water, he would not be silent. The Captain was determined not to have his noise, ordered him to be gaged, which consisted of a piece of rusty Iron placed in his mouth & tied behind his head, a very painful operation soon fetched blood, was in this state for 1 hour & then allowed to have it out, he took care to be quiet enough afterwards, out 40 days.[52]

Despite the enormous loss of life on the maiden run to Melbourne,

---

51 Diary of Edwin Bird 1853 Voyage on Marco Polo to Melbourne NLA MS 6064.
52 Diary of William Culshaw Greenhalgh passenger on board the Marco Polo, 1853. Reproduced in full in Appendix B, Stammers Michael. The Passage Makers. Toredo Books, 1978.

the **Marco Polo** continued to transport emigrants between Liverpool and Melbourne until 1867, making 25 voyages with an incredible consistency in time taken for the round trip. Except for the first voyage to Melbourne, the **Marco Polo** was a relatively healthy vessel. For example, the following report was contained in the Melbourne *Argus* of 30 May 1853:

> The Marco Polo, this renowned clipper ship, arrived yesterday from Liverpool, having made the passage from that port to Hobson's Bay in seventy five days. Another laurel to her already well-earned crown under the able command of Captain Forbes. She has on board seven hundred and fifty passengers, amongst whom not a single case of sickness has occurred; something unparalleled when so large a number of people are in so close contact.

Regarding the next passage by the **Marco Polo**, the story of a passenger who made the voyage as a child arriving in January 1854, was printed in the Melbourne *Argus* on 18 June 1921. Below is an extract from that report:

> After entering Port Phillip Heads, we had the misfortune to run on a sandbank, and the passengers were transferred to a lighter, and taken to Williamstown. Thence I was rowed across to St. Kilda, which at that time consisted of a few scattered houses. Our passenger-list was over 700, my father being ship's surgeon, and we arrived in Melbourne with the same number as when we left there being one death and one birth during the voyage.

Similar comments were made about an 1856 voyage in the Launceston *Cornwall Chronicle* on 10 December 1856:

> The Marco Polo left Liverpool on the 5th September, at 3 p.m. and arrived off Port Phillip heads on Monday last: but owing to the wind shifting to the north, she was unable to enter the port until yesterday. Captain Clarke reports very fine weather, he never had occasion to take in the royal for twenty four hours or reef the topsails during the voyage. The passengers have enjoyed very good health.

Like all wooden vessels of that era, the timber in the *Marco Polo* became more and more strained and waterlogged as time passed. However, she continued to average between 80 and 90 days each way, the last passage home to Liverpool was in fact made in only 76 days. It seems all her captains on the Australia run (Forbes, McDonnell, Wild, Clark, Johnstone and Arnold) drove her hard.

Captain Arnold ca. 1870
(State Library of New South Wales)

In its 15 years of service on the Liverpool–Melbourne run for the Black Ball Line, the *Marco Polo* carried about 15,000 passengers to Australia and most arrived in a healthy condition. The *Marco Polo* developed a reputation as a fast-sailing vessel and the appalling death toll on the first passage was soon forgotten by most of the people of Melbourne. It was probably a sad day when, in 1867, she failed her passenger survey and was forced to return to being a cargo carrier.

While the *Marco Polo* made lots of fast passages to Melbourne, they were certainly not uneventful. Clearly the first passage was a disaster because of the overcrowding, the disease and the deaths that followed. Because she sailed in the Great Southern Ocean, there was damage to rigging and sails and great discomfort to the passengers. She also went aground twice and was involved in minor collisions. There was a fire in the galley on the second voyage which was fortunately extinguished before it could spread. The greatest trauma occurred on 7 March 1871 when the **Marco Polo** struck an iceberg on the way home to Liverpool, causing severe damage to the forward part of the ship. Although leaking badly, she was successfully sailed to Valparaiso, Chile, where repairs were carried out.

The image below is a close-up of an inscription on part of a silver tea set presented to Captain Charles Ferguson. It reads as follows: 'Presented by the owners of the Marco Polo to Captain Charles Ferguson, Harbour Master of Melbourne Victoria. To mark their high estimation of his invaluable services in rescuing their favourite and far-famed ship from her perilous position when stranded in Port Phillip Bay in January last. Liverpool July MDCCCLIV.'

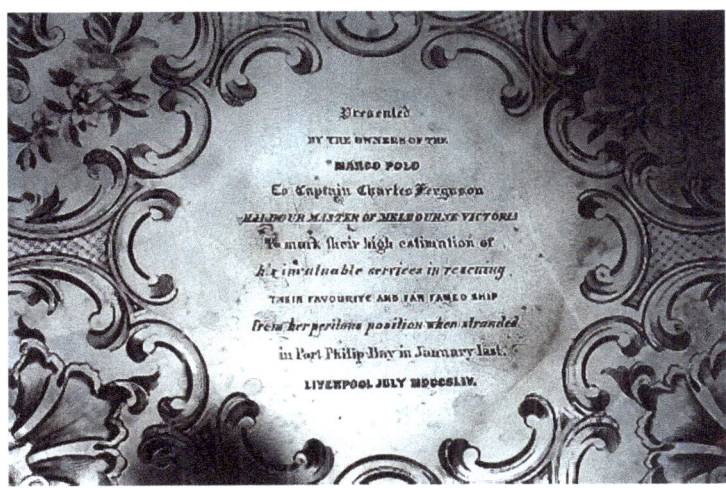

Inscribed Silver Tea Service
(new-brunswick.net)

The Black Ball Line sold the **Marco Polo** when she failed her passenger survey in 1867. For the next 16 years she carried cargo to various parts of the world. On 22 July 1883, caught in a furious gale and leaking badly, she was deliberately driven onto the shore at Cavendish, Prince Edward Island, by the captain (Captain Bull). She lay on her side for some time and during a further fierce storm broke up, marking the end of the *Marco Polo*.

Marco Polo **by D M Little**
(Note: this painting of the Marco Polo
shows the stern of the vessel with the carvings)
(State Library of Victoria)

Chapter 8

THE *TICONDEROGA*

Thou, too sail on, O Ship of State!
Sail on, O Union, strong and great!
Humanity with all its fears,
With all the hopes of future years,
Is hanging breathless on thy fate!
Henry Wadsworth Longfellow[53]

THE ***TICONDEROGA*** WAS a four-masted American double-decker ship of 1089 tons. She was built in Williamsburgh (later the 'h' was dropped), New York, by Perrine, Patterson and Starch in 1849. They had established the shipyard in 1845 at the foot of North Second Street (now named Metropolitan Avenue). The partnership broke up in 1853 (Stark continued on his own), but not before they had constructed almost 50 vessels, including ferries, packets, schooners, barkentines and clippers.

---

53   American poet Henry Wadsworth Longfellow was captivated by the building of the large clipper ships, spent much time watching construction & writing poems about them.

Williamsburg Waterfront & Harbour 1850

The ***Ticonderoga*** was different from the other vessels they had built. She was described as a clipper-like ship constructed of oak and iron and the hull was copper fastened. It seems the ***Ticonderoga*** was put to work soon after her launch on the Atlantic route, taking goods (including cotton) to England and returning with some passengers (probably many were Irish) and cargo. She was registered to the Black Star Line, which carried a crimson swallow tail flag with a black ball in the centre on its vessels and had run packet vessels between New York and Liverpool for a number of years. The ***Ticonderoga*** was also destined to spend her time as another packet vessel. However, she was the fourth of the North American–built vessels to be chartered in 1852 by the Emigration Commission to take emigrants to the colonies. Before being chartered, she had already made two Atlantic crossings between New York and Liverpool in the first part of 1852.

The *Salisbury and Winchester Journal*, on Saturday, 26 June 1852, speculated on the reasons for the Emigration Commission chartering the ***Ticonderoga***:

Government and the Shipowners – Within the last few days the Ticonderoga, an American vessel of 1,100 tons register, has been chartered by the Government Emigration Commissioners to take out emigrants to Australia from this port. Some persons assert that this employment of a foreign vessel was an act of necessity, resulting from the scarcity of suitable British ships; others state that a preference was given to the Ticonderoga because her owners accepted rather lower sum per head for the emigrants than a British owner would take.

On 4 August 1852 the ***Ticonderoga*** departed Birkenhead, Liverpool, with 795 emigrants, predominantly Highland Scots (634), some English (140) from Somerset and Gloucestershire, and a small number of Irish (21). Thirty-four of the Scots had been chosen and supported by the Highland and Emigration Society. The ***Ticonderoga*** emigrants were mainly shepherds and farmworkers from a rural background who had been through difficult times and were looking forward to a new and better life in the colony of Victoria. In addition to the passengers, there were 57 crew members, comprising five officers, 30 able seamen, 15 ordinary seamen and seven others (cooks, carpenters and stewards).

As the Birkenhead depot could only accommodate 400 passengers at a time, the processing of the 795 emigrants on the ***Ticonderoga***, as with the other large double- deck vessels, must have been done in at least two groups. Processing and embarkation usually took four days and so, for 795 passengers, the process would have been spread out over eight or more days. The four-day process usually involved a free day (day three) to correct any problems or deficiencies. During this time passengers were permitted to go into town if they wished, which provided an opportunity for them to be exposed to any infectious diseases present in the local community. This was possibly a particular problem for a number of the emigrants departing on this voyage as many came from rural communities and, having not been exposed to the diseases of the port towns before, hadn't achieved any level of immunity. It's also possible the second group waiting admission to the Birkenhead depot would have arrived a few days before admission and been accommodated in the community, offering opportunities for exposure to infectious diseases prevalent in that community. The need to process passengers in two groups was possibly a significant disadvantage in using the larger vessels like the ***Ticonderoga***.

The vessel was captained by Thomas H. Boyle, with Dr J. C. Sanger as the surgeon superintendent and Dr James William Henry Veitch as assistant surgeon. Captain Boyle was Irish born and a part owner in the vessel. Part ownership of nineteenth- century vessels was common as this encouraged the captains to ensure the success of a voyage and particularly to secure passengers and cargo for the return passage. There was also a matron for the voyage to take care of the single women.

The vessel was well provisioned for the passage to Victoria. Provisions included over 34,300 pounds of flour, 10,304 pounds of split peas, 10,550 pounds of sugar, over 6,000 pounds of raisins, barrels of navy bread, preserved beef and pork, canned soup, over 400 gallons of pickles, 7,000 pounds of treacle, 24,800 pounds of oatmeal and seven chests of tea.

Under normal circumstances, the voyage should have been a relatively uneventful one, with passengers experiencing a wide range of weather conditions and only the occasional bout of seasickness.

From the outset there were problems associated with the double-decker aspect of the ship. Poor ventilation and lighting were the major two, and this was particularly the case for those accommodated on the second deck. There were no water closets on the second deck, which meant passengers on that deck had to move up to the first deck or utilise the 'night utensils' they had been provided with prior to embarkation. Washing the decks wasn't commonly practiced as the water would leak from deck to deck and it was almost impossible to eliminate the damp conditions the steerage passengers were subjected to. The whale oil used in the lamps had an unpleasant odour. The personal hygiene of passengers was observed at a very basic level, at least by contemporary standards. There were approximately 40 babies and toddlers on board, and this meant noise from crying and smells from nappies and the vomit. As was usual on any passage to the colonies in the nineteenth century, there were also passengers suffering from seasickness. The atmosphere between decks grew more and more unpleasant and polluted as the voyage proceeded. At night the hatches were battened down, trapping the smells below the main deck. The crew member opening the hatches in the morning must have been confronted by very unpleasant odours emerging from below.

The risk of disease was heightened by a lack of space for exercise on the upper deck, poor personal hygiene, an aversion to medical treatment and ignorance about the incubation of disease that existed amongst many of the passengers. There is no doubt any infection or 'fever' would thrive amongst such shocking sanitary conditions and the proximity of passengers due to the overcrowding.

Even the second-class passengers who were in shared cabins complained about the overcrowding. The cabins allocated to them accommodated four passengers, but they were very small—about the size of a cabin for a single person. Hence the cabin passengers were also travelling in grossly overcrowded accommodation.

Within about two weeks into the passage, signs of typhus were evident (red rashes, fever, diarrhoea and finally delirium). Within a month, the problem had increased significantly, approaching an epidemic.

Tragically, the first death occurred on 12 August, only eight days at sea. It was that of a baby who died of marasmus (wasting away, probably from malnutrition). It was not uncommon for babies to die in this way on emigrant vessels taking passengers to the colonies. On 9 September two women committed suicide; one was the mother of the baby that had died of marasmus.

On the latter part of the passage in the Great Southern Ocean, the passengers suffered terribly from the extreme cold and dampness. They encountered storms involving strong winds, sleet, heavy rain and some snow. In these storms enormous waves would break over the ship and flood the upper deck, allowing water to stream through every crack and opening down to the lowest parts of the ship. On that part of the voyage passengers and crew were without dry clothing, often soaked to the skin and freezing. Unable to keep warm and often already sick, people died daily.

One hundred of the *Ticonderoga* passengers perished on the voyage; 17 adult males, 29 adult females, 39 children between one and 14 years of age and 15 infants under the age of one year. It appears crew members also became sick and were unable to perform their duties, which led to a breakdown of shipboard routines. The cooking rosters also broke down and food preparation was neglected. Thus, those that died did so amongst an increasing level of mould and squalor found on board after the ship arrived.

There are differences in the records relating to the main cause of the deaths. It's clear scarlatina was a significant cause of death and typhus was present on an epidemic scale. Typhus continued to be a significant problem after arrival. Although it was not known at that time lice spread typhus, the conditions on board the *Ticonderoga* were ideal for them to move from body to body. As people suffering from typhus give off an extremely unpleasant pungent odour, the stench from so many typhus sufferers would have been unpleasant to the point of being nauseating. In fact, another common name for typhus was putrid fever.

In rough weather it was almost impossible to conduct burials and so bodies were often held until a break in the weather. One passenger described how up to 10 dead passengers were bundled up in bedding and mattresses at a time and thrown overboard to float away. Using the bedding as a cover for bodies became necessary in the latter part of the voyage as the ship's sailmakers had run out of canvas. Iron weights had also become scarce.

There was so much sickness on board that the doctors soon ran out of medical supplies. The captain then provided his medical supplies, but they were soon depleted. The two doctors also became exhausted trying to support over 300 sick people and Dr Sanger began to display the early symptoms of typhus.

On 1 November 1852, 90 days after their departure, in the partial darkness of the early morning light, the Cape Otway light was sighted. After such a horrendous passage and with so much sickness still onboard, this must have been a moment of relief and hope for passengers and crew. Later that morning the ***Ticonderoga*** hove to outside the heads and requested assistance from a pilot to guide the vessel through the area known as the Rip. The pilot cutter, ***Ranger***, arrived to provide assistance. It's not clear if she sailed into Port Phillip Bay on 1 November or if it occurred later. The ***Ticonderoga*** was directed to Shortlands Bluff (now Queenscliff), where she waited until directed to Point Nepean, where she apparently dropped anchor on 3 November. Point Nepean had been nominated as a site for a quarantine station.

Old Map of Port Phillip Bay showing Point Otway, Melbourne & Geelong
(Note: Queenscliff is located just inside Port Phillip Bay on the left and the quarantine site at Point Nepean is just inside the Bay on the right)
(State Library of Victoria)

The *Argus* reported on Tuesday 9 November 1852 the Port and Harbour Master at Williamstown, Captain Charles Ferguson, said:

> *100 deaths and nineteen births had occurred on the passage, seven of the former since the ship anchored at the Heads. There are at present 300 cases of sickness amongst them, principally scarlatina.*

There were in fact 311 cases of fever (defined as typhus), 127 cases of diarrhoea and 16 cases of dysentery on the ship's arrival.

The arrival was also reported to the people of Melbourne in the *Argus* on 5 November as follows:

> *Intelligence was brought to Williamstown on Wednesday evening last, by Captain Wylie, of the brig Champion from Adelaide, that a large ship, named the Ticonderoga, ninety days out from Liverpool, with upwards of 900 government emigrants on board, had anchored at the Heads. A great amount of sickness had occurred among the passengers, more than a hundred deaths having taken place, and almost a similar number of cases (typhus fever) being still on board. Nor was this all. The doctor's health was so precarious that he was not expected to survive, and the whole of the medicines, medical comforts. &c, had been consumed. The authorities in Williamstown, immediately furnished the government schooner Empire, with the necessary supplies of livestock, beef, mutton, milk, vegetables, porter, wine, spirits, and a medicine chest, and Dr. Taylor, of the Ottillia, a gentleman of much practical experience, went down in her to the Ticonderoga yesterday, to take charge, accompanied by Captain Ferguson, the Harbour Master. The Lysander ship has also been taken up by Government as a Quarantine Hulk, and proceeds to her destination at the Heads this day, having on board stores sufficient for all hands for three months, when further, arrangements will be made, which we trust will ameliorate the fearful state of things on board. The foregoing are the only particulars known to our reporter at present, but at*

all events, this case clearly exhibits the cruelty and ill-judged policy of crowding such a number of people on board a single ship, no matter her size, for a lengthened voyage.

The report given by the Immigration Board in Melbourne to the Emigration Commissioners in London on the condition of the ***Ticonderoga*** on its arrival, stated:

The ship, especially the lower part was in a most filthy state, and did not appear to have been cleaned for weeks, the stench was overpowering, the lockers so thoughtlessly (?) provided for the Immigrants use were full of dirt, mouldy bread, and suet full of maggots, beneath the bottom boards of nearly every berth upon the lower deck were discovered soup and bouilli cans and other receptacles full of putrid ordure, and porter bottles etc, filled with stale urine, while maggots were seen crawling underneath the berths, and this state of things must have been prevalent for a long time as the 2nd Mate describes the ship to have been in the same state when he supervised the cleaning of her by the Captain's order five weeks previously.[54]

The description of conditions on the ship given by Dr Hunt, the Port Health Officer, had a similar impact but wasn't as dramatic:

The great mortality seems to have been occasioned by the crowded state of her decks and want of proper ventilation, particularly through the lower deck; this caused debility and sickness among her passengers to such an extent that a sufficient number could not be found to keep them clean; dirt and filth of the most loathsome description accumulated, tainting the atmosphere and affecting everyone who came within its influence, as with a poison.[55]

---

54 Report of the Immigration Board, Melbourne upon the Ship 'Ticonderoga' 25 January 1853.
55 Annual Report of the Health Officer, Thomas Hunt, 1 May 1852 to 30 June 1853, p. 3. Parliament of Victoria GP V 1853/54 no. A42.

The *Ticonderoga* was officially placed in quarantine on 5 November and the yellow flag was hoisted. Prior to that, Captain Boyle was instructed to land the *Ticonderoga* at Point Nepean. In order to accommodate the *Ticonderoga* passengers, a quarantine ground was quickly marked out with yellow flags and white paint on the trees, and tents were erected using the sails and spars from the ship. The government purchased two houses that had been occupied by lime-burners and converted them into hospitals. The captain, doctors and those of the crew who were able began moving the sick on 3 November. More of the sick were unloaded on each day for several days. The Government schooner *Empire* arrived on 5 November with food and medical supplies. The *Lysander*, which had been hired by the government to act as a quarantine ship, was dispatched to Point Nepean to act as a hospital ship. The joiners from the *Ticonderoga* were employed to quickly undertake a fit-out to accommodate 50 of the most serious cases.

Quarantine Ground Port Phillip Bay ca. 1851 by Thomas Ham
(State Library of Victoria)

By this stage in the drama, doctors Sanger and Veitch were also in a debilitated state, particularly the former as he had contracted typhus during the voyage. Another doctor, Joseph Taylor, was quickly found to take up the position of medical officer in charge of the new quarantine station. He had been the surgeon superintendent of the ship *Ottillia* and he arrived with the supplies on board the *Empire*. The two doctors from the *Ticonderoga* were so incapacitated and fatigued they were unable to provide any assistance to Dr Taylor. A Dr Farman, who had been the surgeon on the ship *Mobile*, was recruited to assist with the cases on the *Lysander*. However, he was subsequently dismissed because of charges of drunkenness against him and a Dr Sewell was then recruited to take his place.

Despite the provisions and medical attention, a further 68 passengers died in quarantine. Two further crew members also died, bringing the casualty total to 168 souls who lost their lives either on the voyage or later during quarantine. Out of the 307 male passengers, 69 died. Out of the 339 female passengers, 99 died. Among the dead were 86 children, of which 23 were infants under a year old. It's amazing considering the large number of infant deaths that 19 babies born during the voyage appear to have survived.

The Port Health Officer, Dr Hunt, made the following comment about the death rate:

> The 'Ticonderoga' having left Liverpool with 811 souls on board, reported upon entering Port Phillip Heads, 96 deaths, giving a percentage of 11.83 deaths on the voyage. Before her quitting the Sanctuary Station at Point Nepean, where she was detained six weeks, her deaths amounted to 178, a total per cent of 21.95 deaths.[56]

The ship was released from quarantine on 19 December 1852 and deaths that occurred after this date were not considered as having

---

56 Annual Report of the Health Officer, Thomas Hunt, 1 May 1852 to 30 June 1853, footnote p. 7. Parliament of Victoria GP V 1853/54 no. A42.

taken place during the voyage or while in quarantine. The number of these deaths is not known because there were no statutory records but at least 10 further deaths can be reliably inferred from contemporary sources. Re-embarkation was a slow process because there was no jetty. While a few passengers still suffering from typhus were retained on the ***Lysander***, most of the surviving passengers arrived in Melbourne on 22 December, although in a poor state of health and without one or more of their family members. Being a large vessel, the ***Ticonderoga*** anchored in Hobsons Bay and waited for the usual light craft to arrive and transport the passengers up the Yarra Yarra River to Queen's Wharf. This did not occur immediately because of rumours about the ship being a carrier of yellow fever, which was greatly feared at that time. On Friday 24 December the captain and crew of the paddle steamer ***Maitland*** agreed to ferry the passengers up the Yarra.

Hobson's Bay and Williamstown, Port Phillip ca. 1850
(created by Ham brothers engravers)
(State Library of Victoria)

Several trips were made on the ***Maitland*** and the ***Ticonderoga*** passengers were finally in Melbourne. They would have had a sense of despair and grief not experienced by the many new arrivals to Victoria that had preceded them. Their feelings would have contrasted markedly with the excited and eager gold seekers arriving in Melbourne. Docking at the time of the gold rush most probably meant the ***Ticonderoga*** passengers would have encountered further disadvantages because of an accommodation shortage and high prices for goods and food.

The *Argus* published an article entitled 'A heartrending scene' on 28 December 1852 describing the passengers at Queen's Wharf:

On their landing at the wharf, the majority of them seemed in a deplorable condition from debility and sickness, the females especially looking most emaciated and feeble, and many required assistance to the drays which conveyed them to the Immigration Depot. Whilst the steamer was coming up the river one poor little child died of fever, whilst, on the boat arriving in Melbourne, its mother was engaged in laying out the body of her child on the deck, having left, we hear, her husband on board ship, still suffering from fever. Another female was carried from the vessel, apparently in a dying state, it being doubted whether she would ever reach her destination alive. The disgust and astonishment, mingled with the greatest sympathy, that these poor unfortunate passengers should have been sent on shore while still in so weak and sickly a state was loudly expressed by spectators of the scene at the wharf.

Queens Wharf, Melbourne 1850s by S.T. Gill
(State Library of Victoria)

The impact of so many deaths in so many families would have been felt by friends and relatives both in the home country and the colonies. There are doubtless many stories of grieving families as a result of what took place on the *Ticonderoga* passage to Melbourne and afterwards during quarantine. An example of this is contained in a story carried in the Melbourne *Argus* on Saturday 4 August 1934, contributed by a *Ticonderoga* descendant, John Andrew McIvor, entitled 'Whose Names are Unknown':

> *Returning in leisurely fashion from Haymarket, in Melbourne, to the scattered cottages of Coburg, Grandfather McIvor (He was my grandfather) recalled in Gaelic such news as he had gathered. His neighbours – all new settlers – heard with concern of the fever-ship and wondered what friends and neighbours from their native towns overseas might be among the thousand souls said to have embarked in her at Birkenhead.*
>
> *For eight weeks the ill-starred ship swung at anchor inside Point*

Nepean. The fever raged among her company in spite of all measures of relief; vague rumours reached Melbourne that deaths were still occurring at the rate of two and three a day. These were confirmed by a doctor who returned. The rumour that the infection was yellow fever was contradicted and it was declared to be scarlatina, but many survivors afterwards maintained that it was the dreaded 'yellow jack' of the American southern coast. They gained some support from the fact that the ship had traded in those regions on previous voyages, and from the high mortality attending the outbreak.[57]

No passenger list was available in Melbourne. The unfortunate new arrivals were remote as though on a desert island; but a few days before Christmas a young stranger stood at Grandmother McIvor's door at Coburg, and said, 'your cousin, the wife of Malcolm McRae, came on the ship Ticonderoga. I am her son, but my sister Janet, and my two young brothers died of fever since we were landed at Point Nepean, and I have walked from the place with another young man, and we follow the beach till we came to Melbourne.' So there was young McRae, at the end of a 60-mile walk, during which he saw few white people, but one or two black fellows gathering shell-fish. Granny, with many exclamations (in Gaelic) brought him inside and sat him down to the table, bringing forward new scones and buttermilk, and a large round pat of butter stamped with a thistle design. And as she did so, she mourned for little Janet and the two boys, and asked many anxious questions about her cousin Helen - all the way from Inverness, and only 60 miles away now! Alas, they never met!

This is but one of many stories relating to the suffering and grief caused by the many deaths that occurred on the ***Ticonderoga*** during

---

57   Yellow Fever commonly, referred to as Yellow Jack, was a disease common in a number of countries including North America during the eighteenth and nineteenth centuries. It was thought be an infectious disease until it was discovered in the 1880s that it was a virus transmitted by mosquitos.

the voyage and while in quarantine. Because there were many Scots on that voyage, there must have been much sadness in many towns and villages in Scotland once the news of the deaths was received. An interesting Scottish connection is made by Cristina McAskell, writing about the Scots who died on the ***Ticonderoga*** in the *Age, Weekend Magazine* on 17 June 1939. She points out the word Ticonderoga became a part of Scottish folk lore after a battle between the French and English in 1758. On 17 July of that year a Major Duncan Campbell and 500 Scots from the Old Highland Regiment died at Fort Carillon on the Great Lakes, now part of the state of New York. Campbell had told his fellow soldiers sometime prior to the battle he had a dream he would die at a place called Ticonderoga (unknown to him or his companions). His place of death at the French entrenchment was known by the local North American Indians as Ticonderoga. At an old cemetery on Lake George, New York State, there is a headstone with the following epitaph:

> *Here lyes the body of*
> *Duncan Campbell, of Inverawe,*
> *Major of the Old Highland Regiment*
> *Age 55 years*
> *Who died 17 July, 1758 of wounds received*
> *At the attack on the entrenchment of*
> *Ticonderoga.*

Thus, the word Ticonderoga became associated with death.

Although three of the other double-deck ships had already arrived in Victoria before the arrival of the ***Ticonderoga***, this was the most tragic voyage. While the substantial loss of life on board the other three was viewed with alarm, the incredible loss of life on the ***Ticonderoga*** was seen as shocking by the Emigration Commission and again called into question their judgement in using these large vessels and in allowing so many children on board.

Since 1952, the bay between Observatory Point and Police Point on the Nepean Peninsula has borne the name of Ticonderoga and a memorial to those who lost their lives on this ill-fated vessel lies in the Point Nepean Cemetery. The bodies on board on arrival and those who died during quarantine were buried in a temporary cemetery near the beach, but this proved unsuitable and a new site was selected further down the peninsula. Most of the remains from that early cemetery were moved to the new cemetery some years later. The experience with the *Ticonderoga* demonstrated that an adequate quarantine facility was urgently required at Point Nepean and thus a building program commenced, starting with a wooden hospital to accommodate 50 patients.

The *Ticonderoga* sailed out of Hobsons Bay on 15 January 1853 to the heads where she was anchored for the night. The next morning she sailed out through the Rip bound for Akyab, Burma, never to return to Port Phillip. It appears the *Ticonderoga* finished her days as a cargo vessel. She was sold to an Indian merchant in 1863 and was then engaged in transporting cargo around Asian ports. The end came for the *Ticonderoga* on 25 October 1872 when she was wrecked on the east coast of India (along the Bay of Bengal), also known as the Puri coast, which is part of the Indian state of Odisha (then Orissa), some 23 years after being launched in New York.

Chapter 9

THE *BEEJAPORE*

The finest wooden sailing-ships were built upon my shore,
The roaring "Marco Polo" and the bounding "Beejapore";
The "Flying Cloud", the "Guiding Star",
and other far-famed ships,
Designed and built by St. John men,
went smoking from their ships.

The Port of St. John, H.A. Cody

THE ***BEEJAPORE*** WAS a 1676 ton full-rigged clipper-style vessel built at Saint John, New Brunswick, in 1851 by William and Richard Wright. By 1839 the Wright brothers had established their own shipbuilding yard at Courtenay Bay, Saint John. During their first eight years of operation, they built 15 vessels, averaging 567 tons in size.

Typical Ship Construction
(*Revolving Light* - **1338 tons**) **New Brunswick**
(New Brunswick Museum – Musée du Nouveau-Brunswick,
www.nbm-mnb.ca, 19151)

A number of the vessels were built for sale or on order for merchants. The Wright brothers retained some of the vessels for a short period before selling them, often in Liverpool, after delivering a cargo of timber. In 1847 they moved into ship owning by retaining two of the three ships they built that year, both vessels being the first they constructed that exceeded 1000 tons. This marked the start of a period during which they were noted for being the builders of the largest class of wooden ships. Their next 15 ships averaged 1352 tons. The last two ships, the ***White Star*** (2339 tons) in 1854 and the ***Morning Light*** (2379 tons) in 1855, were the largest sailing ships built at that time. The Wrights operated many of their ships, not from the port of registration, but from Liverpool.

Market Slip, Saint John, New Brunswick
(New Brunswick Museum – Musée du Nouveau-Brunswick,
www.nbm-mnb.ca, 9692)

The ***Beejapore***, at 1676 tons, was one of these very large vessels that emerged from the Wright shipyard. She was classified as a ship with three decks (main and two below) and three masts.

In 1852 the Emigration Commissioners chartered the ***Beejapore***, the fifth of the large North American–built vessels, to transport 967 souls (equivalent to 775 statute adults) to New South Wales at a cost of £15 18s 9d per statute adult. She left Liverpool on 12 October 1852 and arrived in Port Jackson on 6 January 1853. The captain was S.L. McLay, the surgeon superintendent was Dr Barnetts and the assistant surgeon was Osborne Johnson.

The emigrants carried by the ***Beejapore*** included many Scottish handloom weavers from Paisley who came as families with a significant number of children. This was a departure from the normal type of emigrant approved by the Emigration Commissioners. A letter from the Secretary to the CLEC, S. Walcott, dated 6 October 1852, was sent to the authorities in New South Wales prior to the departure providing justification and the rationale for this decision. The letter includes the following:

> *I am directed by the Colonial Land and Emigration Commissioners to state to you for the information of the Governor of New South Wales, the circumstances under which the Commissioners have thought themselves justified in sending out to Sydney, a number of Scotch hand-loom Weavers who will reach the Colony in the ship 'Beejapore'.*
>
> *You will doubtless have become aware that the eager demand for a large and immediate supply of emigrants, which was received last June from the Colonies of New South Wales and Victoria, was enforced on the Commissioners if possible, more strongly by those Colonists who happened to be in England, and these Gentlemen pointed out to the Board repeatedly and with much force that the peculiar circumstances of the moment considerably modified the character of Emigrants required. They pointed out that the robust health and the absence of encumbrances and the habit of hard labour, which under ordinary circumstances were the first requisites of a useful Emigrant would under present circumstances render him most likely to betake himself to the diggings, and that the peculiar exigency required not so much industrious and enterprising young men as persons who from age, disposition or any other cause would be likely to prefer the comparatively idle life of tending sheep to the hazards or hardships of seeking Gold.*[58]

The letter went on to further explain how the Scottish weavers fitted the criteria and how this was seen by the Commission as an experiment. The letter also asked if feedback could be provided on the 'propriety of this emigration' and in regard to the emigrants 'of their

---

58 Letter S Wallcott to E. Deas Thomson, 6 January 1853, State Records NSW 53/3960.

steadiness in adhering to their engagements and their usefulness as labourers'. Feedback was eventually provided in April 1853.

The Geelong *Advertiser and Intelligencer* reported on shipping to the colonies on Thursday 6 January 1853:

> EMIGRATION FROM LIVERPOOL. —*The number of ships despatched by the Government officials during the month was 62, containing in all 23,280 passengers, including 1770 emigrants, principally Scotch, from the depot at Birkenhead, all of whom are bound for Australia...Four other vessels are to leave Birkenhead during the present month, the Beejapore, the Priscilla, the Thames, and the Arabine. The Beejapore, which is the largest vessel ever despatched to the antipodes, is now alongside the depot, waiting for her passengers. She will carry about 750 adults, equal to about 920 souls, exclusive of officers and crew...*

On the 1852 passage the **Beejapore** carried 967 assisted immigrants, including 342 children. The number of crew was 65, which means the **Beejapore** carried 1032 people in total. The ship was grossly overcrowded with this number of steerage-class passengers below decks and thus conditions were ideal for the spread of infectious diseases. It was an uncomfortable passage in the cramped conditions that was marked by illness and death. To make things even worse, part of the passage was extremely rough when the vessel struck hurricane-like weather:

> *Friday, December 31*
>
> *...topsail split in three places with a loud report...the sea was now fearfully high, wave after wave rolling towards us...*
>
> *Tuesday 4 January*
>
> *...the ship was rolling very heavily all night and scarcely any got any sleep...*[59]

---

59 Journal of Voyages from England to Australia 1852 to 1856 – Beejapore October 1852–January 1853. NLA Mfm G28208.

According to diarist Johnson (no first name given), the rough weather had started in November and continued periodically during the voyage. Passenger Johnson commented in November and again in January:

> *Sunday Nov 28th Raining constantly all day…towards evening it came on to downright hair blowing weather…some sails taken down but in spite of this we made 11 knots.*
>
> *Monday Jan 3rd Blowing very hard and ship under close reef topsail…*
>
> *Tuesday 4th The ship rolling very heavily…*[60]

Sketch of Ship *Condor* from Johnson Diary passenger on the *Beejapore* (Saturday November 27th, 1852 – NLA MS6118)

Diarist Johnson noted an interaction with the **Condor**, bound for Port Phillip, during the passage and listed in his diary the deaths each day, starting with five in October and then in November and December almost one every day (on some days multiple deaths occurred).

---

60 Journal of Johnson. Voyage from Liverpool to Sydney Oct 1852 to Jan 1853. NLA MS6118.

It seems the ***Beejapore*** was only a few days out when the first death occurred on 16 October:

> *One of the passenger's children died during the night.*[61]

The ***Beejapore*** arrived several miles off Sydney Heads on the evening of Wednesday 5 January 1853, after a passage of 84 days, at 22 hours mean time, and would have been flying the yellow quarantine flag as required by law.

The arrival was reported in the *Sydney Morning Herald* on Thursday 6 January 1853 as follows:

> *The Beejapore, from Liverpool, eighty five days out, was reported from the Signal Station yesterday evening, and we consequently began to make preparations for giving our readers a batch of late English news this morning. We soon, however, learnt that the vessel had sickness on board, and our reporter, who had gone several miles outside the heads to her, was not allowed to approach sufficiently near to obtain newspapers or information. She has upwards of a thousand people on board. We hope to receive some papers from her in the course of the day.*

On arrival the ship was placed in quarantine due to an outbreak of measles on board and the number of deaths that occurred during the passage. During the voyage, 56 emigrants were buried at sea—55 of them children or infants. While the 86 days it took to travel to Australia were considered record-breaking, the passage for those beneath the decks was horrific.

One of the problems that perplexed the colonial government of New South Wales throughout the nineteenth century, in its administration of the port-of-entry, Port Jackson, was the need to encourage the

---

61 Usherwood, W. Journal of a Voyage to Sydney in the ship Beejapore October 1852 to January 1853. State library of New South Wales MLB734 CY117. Saturday 16 October 1852, p. 3.

growth of shipping while requiring all vessels from overseas to observe quarantine regulations.

In the early days of the colony of New South Wales, passengers and crew were quarantined on their ships. In 1814 a decision was made to use land-based quarantine when convicts and guards from the HMS ***Surrey*** were landed near Milsons Point. North Head became the site for quarantine in 1828 and in July of that year the first ship to be quarantined at Spring Cove was a convict ship called the ***Bussorah Merchant***. An outbreak of smallpox had occurred during the long voyage from England and on arrival the convicts and their guards were housed in tents on the shore of the cove. In 1837 the ***Lady MacNaghten***, an immigrant ship, arrived in Port Jackson with passengers and crew already stricken by typhus and scarlet fever on the voyage. Of the 412 immigrants to the colony, 10 adults and 44 children died on the voyage, followed by 14 more during their lengthy quarantine. The quarantine of the ***Lady MacNaghten*** was the catalyst for the establishment of a permanent quarantine station on North Head and following the allocation of funds by the Legislative Council, buildings began to be erected on the site.

On 28 July 1832, the governor, with the advice of the Legislative Council of New South Wales, passed the first Quarantine Act (an Act for subjecting Vessels coming to New South Wales from certain places to the performance of Quarantine), which was despatched to Britain for Royal Assent on 30 October 1832. On 1 October 1832, the Act was supplemented by Quarantine Regulations to be observed in the Harbour of Port Jackson, New South Wales. Under these Regulations, the master of every vessel arriving from overseas was required to provide written answers to questions on a printed form given to him by the harbour pilot so the pilot could establish if the vessel had called at any infected port, communicated with any infected vessel or experienced an outbreak of infectious disease during the voyage. As a further precaution, the ship's surgeon was also required to sign the master's report. Fines of up to £100 were imposed for any breach of the regulations.

A decision in 1838 to appoint the first Health Officer of Port Jackson was a constructive move towards making the port's quarantine regulations less irksome for commerce while making it more effective in protecting public health. His duty was to visit every vessel entering the port (except those from Van Diemen's Land and engaged in the coastal trade) to determine if there was an infectious disease on board. If he was satisfied there was no risk to Sydney's residents, he was authorised to grant admission to pratique (permission to proceed to a Sydney wharf and unload). In all other cases he was provisionally authorised to quarantine the vessel, her passengers, cargo and mail, pending government approval for his action and his recommendations for steps to be taken to eradicate all traces of disease. While undertaking his duties he was aware he was supposed to carry them out with minimum interruption to trade. However, the medical officer in 1853, then Dr Haynes Alleyne, was reminded by the Medical Adviser to the Select Committee on Quarantine Laws that the guiding principle was:

> ...one grand duty he must ever remember – his duty to the public; and if there were the slightest doubt upon his mind, he must give the public and not the ship, the benefit of his doubt.[62]

On 14 December 1841 the Quarantine Act was amended to give the health officers of Sydney's Port Jackson and Melbourne's Port Phillip (where a quarantine station had been established in 1840), power to place vessels in quarantine. The period of quarantine was generally as long as the medical officer believed to be the incubation period of a particular disease. In 1853 this was set at 21 days for smallpox and 14 days for 'ship fever'.[63]

---

62 Report of the Health Officer of Port Jackson for the year 1853, NSW V&P (LC), 1854, vol. 2 p. 856.
63 Report of the Select Committee on Quarantine Laws, evidence of H.G. Alleyne, 28 June 1853 pp. 1–2.

There were often complaints by shipowners, ship captains and doctors and passengers about the delays caused by the quarantine procedures. However, the number of ships involved, and the magnitude of the health officer's task were immense. In 1853 Dr Alleyne visited 569 ships and quarantined 17 because of measles, typhus fever, scarlet fever or smallpox.[64] Some ship masters tried to avoid delays by concealing the outbreak of an infectious disease on board, despite the risk of being detected and the substantial penalties that could be imposed.

When the **Director** arrived from San Francisco on 29 July 1853, Dr Alleyne granted pratique on the basis of the master's assurance there was no sickness of a contagious or infectious nature on board. Subsequently, a child infected with smallpox was discovered. The vessel and her passengers (including several who had already landed) were quarantined at the station for 63 days. The length of the quarantine was probably partly a punitive measure. Part of the problem faced by the health officer was that ship masters and some ship doctors did not understand the infectious nature of some diseases. For example, some people believed once a person was removed from the origin of the disease, that person would recover or the miasma (toxic atmosphere) causing the disease would be dispersed on land. Another disincentive to report illness and death was the practice of paying a gratuity to the surgeon superintendent on immigrant ships calculated on an amount for each immigrant landed alive or in good health. If the performance was regarded as substandard, it could be decided no gratuity would be paid.

The initiative to improve both quarantine accommodation and procedures came when Captain H. H. Browne was appointed as the new Agent for Immigration on 3 June 1851. As the senior immigration official, he considered he was jointly responsible, with the health officer, for the management of the station as part of the immigration

---

64 Report of the Health Officer of Port Jackson for the year 1853, NSW V&P(LC) 1854, vol. 2 pp. 1239–41.

establishment. In Browne's new role, he met each immigrant ship on arrival, subsequently reporting to the Colonial Secretary on the health of the immigrants on board. He monitored any subsequent quarantine, visiting the station frequently. From the time of his appointment, all recommendations about work needed on the station's buildings were submitted to him for his initial approval. In July 1852 Browne directed the colonial architect, E. T. Blacket, to make urgent repairs to buildings and the landing stage and on 27 August 1852 he also requested Blacket to erect a building at the Landing Stage about eight feet long and six feet wide to house an 'apparatus' for the fumigation of mail before despatch to Sydney. On 22 November 1852, his recommendations for substantially increased accommodation and for changes to quarantine procedures were placed before the Executive Council. His proposal for a small gymnasium was immediately approved, but his other building recommendations were referred to the colonial architect for cost estimates. Browne's recommendations in 1852 for more accommodation at the station, which had accompanied his proposal for a code of quarantine instructions, might have languished in the colonial architect's in-tray for an indefinite period, as sometimes happened. However, circumstances surrounding the quarantine of the ***Beejapore*** on 9 January 1853 brought urgency to the recommendations, since the ship carried over 1000 people and the station's buildings could only accommodate about 150.

The following notice was placed in the New South Wales Government Gazette on Tuesday 11 January 1853:

Colonial Secretary's Office,

Sydney, 8th January, 1853.

QUARANTINE.

SEVERAL cases of Fever and Measles having occurred on board the Ship "Beejapore", His Excellency the Governor, General, with the advice of the Executive Council, has deemed it necessary to place the vessel, crew, and passengers, under Quarantine, according to Law, of which all persons are hereby required to take notice accordingly.

The Boundaries of the Quarantine Station, at Spring Cove, are specified in a Proclamation, dated 15th July, 1837.

By His Excellency's Command,

E. DEAS THOMSON.

Dr Alleyne questioned the captain and surgeon superintendent of the **Beejapore** and completed the health officer's proforma report required by New South Wales law (see copy below). Alleyne was aware of the seriousness of the problem and immediately quarantined the vessel in Spring Cove, where he held preliminary discussions with Carroll and the ship's master about quarantine procedures. The quarantine area was divided into two sections, which were called the 'healthy ground' and the 'sick ground'. On the following morning, the ship's surgeon superintendent met Alleyne and Carroll on shore to inspect the four 'black-painted' buildings on the healthy ground, which could accommodate only about 100 people, and the hospital on the sick ground, which could only accommodate about 50 people, and was told that most of the immigrants would have to be housed in tents, since the ship had to be cleared for cleaning. That evening, some of the crew erected seven tents on the sick ground, and on the following day a further 30 tents were erected on the healthy ground. By 12 January, when about 90 tents had been erected, a cabin passenger, William Usherwood, described the station as 'more like a soldiers' encampment than anything'.[65]

HEALTH OFFICER'S REPORT	
Questions to be put by the Health Officer to the Surgeon and Master, or other Person in command of any ship or Vessel arriving in Port Jackson.	
QUESTIONS	**REPLIES**
1. What is the name of the Vessel and Tonnage?	Beejapore 1672 Tons
2. What is the Master's name?	Macleay
3. From whence do you come and when did you sail?	Liverpool 12th October 1852
4. At what Ports have you touched on your passage?	None
5. Did you receive any Cargo or Passengers at the intermediate ports?	No
6. What is the nature of the Cargo, and the number of Officers, Mariners and Passengers?	Merchandise Crew 60 Passengers 979
7. What Vessels have you had intercourse or communication with on your passage, and from whence did they come?	None
8. Have you any, and what Bill of Health?	No
9. Are you aware that any Epidemical, Contagious, or Infectious Disease prevailed at the place from which you sailed, or at any of the places which you have touched, or on board of any Vessel which you have had communication. If so, state where and when.	Measles brought on board before sailing.
10. In the course of your voyage have any Persons on board suffered from sickness of any kind, and what was the nature of such sickness, and when did it prevail? How many Persons were affected by it and have any to them died in the course of the voyage?	80 cases of measles 20 cases of Scarlet Fever 56 deaths. Most of them from measles 1 death this morning from pneumonia
11. How many sick have you now on board, and from what Disease?	13 cases of measles now on board
12. If any sickness prevailed during the passage, state the date of the first and last case?	Measles brought on board the ship during the period of embarkation appeared only after sailing (in a few days after). It has continued without intermission during the whole of the voyage – 13 cases now on board 56 deaths from causes before stated
13. If any of the Crew or Passengers have died during the voyage, state the nature of the Disease of which they died, and the date?	56 deaths from causes before stated
14. Upon the appearance and prevalence of any Disease, was there any unusual state of the weather, which might lead you to suppose its existence to depend rather upon atmospherical causes then upon specific contagion?	No
15. Are you aware of any circumstances, during the passage or at present, which would render it expedient to place the Ship and people in Quarantine?	Yes
16. To the correctness of the foregoing Statements, are you ready to make declaration, if required?	Yes
	Signed Hayes Gibbes Alleyne MD Health Officer January 6th 1853
Source State Records NSW. Colonial Secretary's correspondence 1853. agent for Immigration to Colonial Secretary 4/3200 53/4869.	

Health Officers Proforma Report on the *Beejapore*
(State Records NSW, Agent for Immigration Correspondence 1853 4/3200)

---

65 Usherwood, W.Journal on Voyage to Sydney in Ship Beejapore 1852–53. Tuesday 11 January, p. 64. State library of New South Wales MF CY 1117.

Sick people were landed as quickly as possible and placed under the care of a doctor sent from Sydney. Plans to land the large contingent of single girls were deferred, however, following a visit to the ship by both Alleyne and Browne, when instructions were given that all clothing was to be thoroughly washed before landing. On 12 January, in intermittent rain, about 150 single girls were landed with their luggage, bedding and cooking utensils. On the following morning T. R. Miles, who had been appointed teacher and religious instructor on the voyage, visited their camp and found the clothing and bedding of many had been soaked by torrential rain during the night. On Miles' return to the ship, he gave a 'miserable account' of the conditions on shore but, according to diarist Usherwood, the ship's captain decided, after going on shore, that Miles' account was 'as usual very much exaggerated'[66]. Orders were given for the disembarkation of the remaining single women, despite the tearful pleas of those who were unnerved by the sight of the station, the burial ground and the sentries who, it was incorrectly rumoured, had orders to shoot anyone who strayed beyond the station's boundary pillars.

Clearly there were those passengers who were concerned about being quarantined and isolated from the Sydney community and of the stigma that may be attached to them because of their arrival in the **Beejapore.** Some wrote to the *Sydney Morning Herald* on 19 January 1853 in an attempt to downplay the seriousness of the problem:

Gentlemen

We, certain of the passengers on board the Beejapore, emigrant vessel, now lying in Spring Cove, are anxious that our case should be properly understood by the residents of Sydney & the colony at large.

We are convinced that from the paragraph announcing the arrival of the ship, how much alarm has been needlessly created in the

---

66 Ibid. Friday 14 January, p. 65.

minds of the resident colonists. That, by this time, the sanitary condition of the emigrants must have been held as truly deplorable to themselves, & extremely dangerous to the future health of the colonial population.

Our object in the present communication is, therefore, to disabuse the minds of the population of New South Wales, through the columns of your journal, & have our case brought directly under the consideration of the colonial authorities.

1 During the passage there was only one death from the adult population on board the Beejapore, & that had no connection with contagion or infection.

2 Since being confined to Spring Cove there have been only two deaths among the adult immigrants neither of which arose from infection or contagion.

3 We are divided into two sections —the one on what is known as the sick ground, the other on the healthy ground. Among the immigrants on the latter, amounting to more than 700 individuals, young & old, there is not one case of sickness. Among the population on the former, there are many individuals in a state of perfect health, who have passed from the one section to the other, rather than be separated from their families.

4 The diseases which have manifested themselves among the immigrants have been measles & certain forms of scariatius, which have been confined to the very young.

5 A number of the early deaths among the infant passengers arose from neither one nor the other of the diseases just mentioned, but from causes yet to be enquired into in an investigation about to be opened by the colonial authorities.

6 Under the facts now mentioned we think it extremely hard that

> *we should be confined in this barren spot without receiving any direct information from the colonial authorities as to what line of action they intend to adopt towards us in reference to the period of detention here.*
>
> *7 As we have received no information from the Surgeon Superintendent relative to the instructions he has received from the colonial authorities as to our detention, a matter in which we are all deeply interested, we would humbly request you, or some of your influential & wealthy townsmen, to forward a copy of the quarantine regulations to us for perusal, addressed to the schoolmaster here.*
>
> *8 We possess no data from which to infer at what period we may hope to be removed from this spot.*

Amongst the 62 people who died subsequently on shore was T.R. Miles' 18-year-old daughter, Gabriella, described by diarist W. Usherwood as a 'lovely, popular girl who liked to watch storms and high seas from the top deck while other girls wept in fear below'. In a bitter letter to the Colonial Secretary on 14 January, her grieving father wrote Gabriella had become 'the first victim to the obstinate and imperious conduct of the surgeon superintendent. She had neither infection nor contagion. She was buried on Tuesday last'[67]. Diarist W. Usherwood indicated several times Miles was unliked, unpopular and a trouble maker. An example of this is a diary entry on Sunday 6 February:

> *Mr. Miles read prayers while we were on shore, we have really been so disgusted with his behaviour lately that we could not have attended, he is the most troublesome man I have seen for long and is constantly endeavouring to brew some disturbance, his hatred to the Doctor is extreme and if he can thwart him in any way does it.*[68]

---

67 Miles to Colonial Secretary 14 January 1853. NSW State Archives and Records, Reel 2941, 5/2454.

68 Usherwood, W. Diary of voyage to Sydney on board the *Beejapore* October 1852 – January 1853, P. 72. State Library of New South Wales MLB784 CY117.

In the same letter Miles asked that a medical deputation be sent to the station since there were fears that another few days might increase the number of victims already laid 'in the narrow Burial Ground in Spring Cove'. He reported the drug dispenser, Charles Robinson, had been found intoxicated on the previous night. Miles also wrote: 'Reports on shore are of a shocking kind as regards the moral conduct of some of the married women and men — not men and their wives — and what do the colonial authorities anticipate from 200 single women let loose in the bush where supervision is altogether impossible?'[69]

Miles had been asked at the start of the voyage to compile an ongoing account of the voyage which he apparently undertook with some enthusiasm. This record was referred to by Usherwood, together with comments that indicate there was continuing tension between Miles and the surgeon superintendent, Dr Barnetts:

> *Mr. and Mrs. Miles dined with us again today. Dr. Barnetts and the former had another long discussion, they both appear to be jealous of their rights and privileges, and frequently allude to their instructions. Mr. Miles certainly thinks his power is much greater than it is in reality, which must I think arise from his having been requested to send a report home from the Colonies, detailing the account of the voyage.*[70]

Miles' letter was referred to the Immigration Board, whose members included both Browne and Alleyne. Solemnly, the Board informed the Colonial Secretary that it was aware of the opportunities for 'the commission of irregularities' presented by 'the uncleared nature of the Quarantine Ground as well as the entire absence of any classification of the Immigrants'. There was concern about the morals of the immigrants and so steps were needed to provide protection (if necessary, despite their personal inclinations) and the response involved a complete reorganisation of accommodation.

---

69   IBID. Miles to Colonial Secretary.
70   IBID. Usherwood. 21 November, 1853, p. 28.

In the report Miles had composed during the voyage, he listed in some detail all the matters he found to be inadequate, including the food and accommodation, and the shortcomings of the captain and the surgeon superintendent. The report and a list of charges made by Miles were forwarded to the Immigration Board. Miles claimed the captain was disinterested in the passengers; the care of the sick was undertaken solely by the junior surgeon; there was no interest in food for infants; many died because of lack of proper nourishment; the sick were compelled to stand in the open air for several hours; passengers were deprived of water and rice; cooking utensils were inadequate; provisions were measured out instead of being weighed; single women were allowed to remain on deck in the tropics until 10 pm; butter, coffee, raisins, suet and treacle were withheld from passengers; the surgeon superintendent would not secure the single women's compartment with a lock; and there was 'illegal appropriation on the Medical Comforts'.[71]

Before the **Beejapore** passengers dispersed, they were interviewed by the members of the Immigration Board. William Usherwood noted this as follows:

> *The Emigration Clerks having finished their list yesterday, Capt H.H. Brown, Dr. Alleyne and Mr. Mann the Commissioners of Emigration came on board about 10.30 pm and immediately mustered them one family at a time to enquire if they had any complaints to make – All expressed themselves perfectly satisfied except 12 or 14 Scotchmen who Miles had persuaded to bear him out in his charges, and from the manner in which these men spoke it was very evident there were no complaints of their own, but that they had been tutored by Miles.*[72]

The surgeon superintendent provided a written statement to the

---

71   General Report of Proceedings on Board the Beejapore; treatment of passengers by the Surgeon Superintendent and Captain with the charges made against the latter by John Reid Miles, Schoolmaster and Chaplain. Contained in papers Collected by Sir William Dixon. Mitchell Library DLADD 127.

72   Usherwood, W. Journal of a Voyage to Sydney in the Ship *Beejapore* October 1852 to January 1853. State Library of New South Wales MLB784 CY117.12 February 1853, p. 73.

chairman and members of the Immigration Board, addressing each of the claims made by Miles. It appears the charges were dismissed by the Board.

As a result of the deficiencies in the quarantine station, revealed by the arrival of the ***Beejapore***, further work proceeded there and by July 1853, the colonial architect had a team of workmen encamped at the station. Under the new plan, people who were suffering from an infectious disease and who had previously been accommodated on the sick ground, were now to be placed on board a hospital ship moored in Spring Cove. Another building was erected on the former sick ground, renamed 'the Point', which then became the place where single women were housed under the watchful eye of a matron. A double line of fencing with two gates was erected around the buildings, where a constable was stationed between the fences to prevent any contact with the single women during a quarantine. Two more buildings were erected on the healthy ground, each accommodating about 60 people, and verandahs were added on three sides of all buildings, so people could eat under shelter.

In place of the former hospital buildings, the hulk ***Harmony*** (a vessel of 600 tons) was purchased for £1600 in 1853 and refitted as a hospital ship and then moored in Spring Cove. Dr Alleyne had not been included in any discussions of the new buildings; indeed, his request to architect Blacket to view the plans was refused. He was consulted, however, about the conversion of the ***Harmony*** into a hospital ship. A floor was laid on the bottom of the ship to provide a second deck, with a height from floor to ceiling of 8 feet, and an upper deck with a height of 6 feet 10 inches. Each deck was divided into two wards, providing accommodation for 60–70 beds that could be used to separate sexes and various types of diseases. Additionally, there were compartments for a surgeon, wardsmen and nurses; a room for compounding medicines; a cookhouse; and 'every requisite for a well-arranged hospital'. Somewhat optimistically, Browne informed a Select Committee on Quarantine Laws on 12 August 1853 the improvements would provide permanent accommodation for 700–800 people 'with great ease'.

More realistically, Alleyne placed the figure at about 450 people, with the hospital ship housing a further 60–70 people.

The changes at the station had included the selection of a new site for a second burial ground, following a report from J. White, clerk of works, that the first burial ground was: 'just below the Healthy Station and so conspicuous that Parties cannot go out to take the fresh air, without being reminded of the mortality of so many placed in similar circumstances to themselves; besides which the water which supplies the Station trickles thru the Grave Yard on one side and the association is anything but agreeable'. On 23 May 1853 the Executive Council directed 'the fencing of the present Burial Ground be entirely removed and the surface of the ground levelled and the gravestones now standing should be carefully transferred to the new ground but that the remains of the dead interred there should not be disturbed'.

The second burial ground was located in the bush behind the buildings on the healthy ground. It was dedicated as a Church of England cemetery on 26 September 1872, when trustees were also appointed. Burials at the station were hasty affairs from which any friends or relatives on the healthy ground were excluded to prevent the risk of infection. Generally, the bodies were carried to their graves by convalescent immigrants, or the people appointed to assist the doctor in charge. Until 1881, there was no formal service at the time of burial.

Quarantine Burial Ground, Port Jackson
(State Library of Victoria)

The period of quarantine was a tale of profound misery—800 immigrants accommodated on shore in crowded conditions (most in tents) with 62 deaths at the quarantine station from measles, scarlet fever and typhus fever in addition to the 56 deaths that had taken place at sea.

The arrival of the ***Beejapore*** demonstrated how ill equipped the North Head Quarantine Station was to handle the volume of ships arriving due to the increasing demand for immigrants in New South Wales.

By the end of the 34-day quarantine of the ***Beejapore,*** the death rate of the sick was over 60 per cent, which indicated the hospital treatment was precarious rather than effective. Of the 62 who died at North Head, 10 were adults and the rest children, with typhoid fever the major cause. Of the total number who embarked on the passage to Sydney on the ***Beejapore***—comprising 624 adults and 305 children plus 40 crew—12 adults and 106 children died.

The period of quarantine was long and most of the passengers longed for it to be over. When the end of quarantine was advised, there was still one more task to perform and one more day to be served before the release:

> *The Health Officer was on board today having at length released us from the miseries of quarantine after 33 days trial thereof, which is I am sure quite sufficient time for anyone to judge, I sincerely trust I may never have to undergo such another trial again. The Pilot was also down just after the Health Officer having been sent down by Mr. Towns who expected the ship would go up direct, but Mr. Carroll the Superintendent here will not clear us until everything is put in the same order as we found it, the ground thoroughly swept and all the rubbish burnt.*[73]

The **Beejapore** was part of the experiment to move large numbers of emigrants quickly and reduce migration costs by using a two-deck vessel. While these goals were probably met, the outcome for many individuals and families who travelled on the **Beejapore** was a disaster.

After a little over two months in port, the **Beejapore** left Port Jackson on 18 March and headed for Callao, Peru. It's not known if she departed with all the original crew as, after the quarantine period had expired, about half the crew indicated they wanted to remain in the colony, possibly influenced by the lure of gold. This was reported in the *Sydney Morning Herald* on Monday 14 February 1853:

> DOMESTIC INTELLIGENCE.
>
> *WATER POLICE OFFICE. —On Friday, nineteen seamen belonging to the emigrant ship Beejapore were brought before the Superintendent of Police and Captain Darley, charged with combining with each other to neglect duty. Mr. Robert Johnson, who conducted the prosecution, stated that these men had during the*

---

73 Usherwood, W. Diary of Voyage to Sydney on the *Beejapore* October 1852 – January 1853. 8 February, p. 72. State Library of New South Wales MLB784 CY117.

whole of the voyage, and during the time that the ship remained in quarantine in Port Jackson, behaved in a very exemplary manner, but upon the ship being brought down to the wharf on Wednesday, they began to evidence a very different spirit; and on Thursday morning upon being called to turn-to by the boatswain, they one and all refused to do so, and expressed their firm determination to do no more duty on board the ship. They were remonstrated with both by the captain and chief officer, but without effect. They assigned no reason for their misconduct; but it was clear from most of them having their clothes packed up, that it was their design to leave the ship if possible. Under these circumstances, the aid of the Water Police was sought, and the men lodged in custody. Mr. Johnson added that, as the conduct of the crew had been so good hitherto, and as it was clear they were now acting under some unfortunate infatuation, Captain McLay would not ask for the punishment of hard labor to be included in any sentence of imprisonment which the bench might think proper to inflict. The charge was fully proved by Captain McLay, and the chief officer, and by the requisite entries in the official log-book. The prisoners declined to ask any, save one or two irrelevant questions, and offered no defence. They each declared that under no circumstances whatever would they do another day's duty on board. Both Mr. McLerie and Captain Darley addressed the men in feeling terms upon the reckless folly of their conduct, and urged on the desirability, for their own sakes of reconsidering their decision, between the gaol and their ship; but in vain. The bench said that under these circumstances they could not entertain Mr. Johnson's kind suggestion in respect to excluding the punishment of hard labour from the sentence; and therefore, ordered that each prisoner be confined in Darlinghurst Gaol for twelve weeks, and there kept to hard labour; at the expiration of that time, to be put on board their ship by the police.

The ***Beejapore*** made another voyage to Sydney in 1857. Although the Emigration Commission had declared that it would not use double-deck vessels again, it appears from media reports this passage involved the transportation of 'Government immigrants'. However, this may have meant the emigrants were sponsored or arrived under bounty arrangements. It's also possible the commissioners were convinced significant improvements had been made to the ***Beejapore*** and if she carried a smaller number of passengers (including less children) she would be an acceptable vessel to transport emigrants to the colonies. An example of the favourable press announcements of her arrival was the report in the *Freeman's Journal* on Saturday 21 March 1857 as follows:

SYDNEY LABOUR MARKET.

Since my last, the Beejapore; has arrived with Government Immigrants, mostly English, consisting of married couples, agricultural labourers, and persons, married or single, belonging to about twenty-four other occupations. On Thursday the hiring commenced; and, from their general appearance, it is not too much to say that they are mostly a well-behaved and respectable class of people, well selected, and creditable to the Surgeon- Superintendent who appears to have been very attentive to them on their- passage. They will doubtless prove a valuable acquisition to the colony just now.

There is no account of that passage to Sydney, nor any record of disease or death on the voyage. She had departed from Southampton on 2 December 1856 under the command of Captain Drenning and carried only 169 passengers. With a small number of passengers in such a large vessel, there would have been lots of space and only a need to use the first deck below the main deck. The departure port was not Liverpool—a port the emigration commissioners had identified as a problem because of disease transmission to the passengers who were on the 1852–1853 passage to Sydney. There was no mention of the need for quarantine when the *Beejapore* arrived in March, so it's likely the passage was uneventful.

In 1863 the *Beejapore* made a third trip to the colonies and took passengers to Keppel Bay, Queensland. By 1863 she was part of the Black Ball Line, still under the command of Captain Drenning and registered to carry only 600 passengers. However, this number was exceeded on the passage to Queensland and the vessel was again overcrowded. As the Emigration Commission was not involved in this voyage—because the Queensland Government was responsible for attracting emigrants using emigration agents and a scheme that offered financial incentives to emigrants or sponsors—the number of passengers assigned to the *Beejapore* was presumably not policed. The surgeon superintendent was Dr Belinfante, a German medico who was reported to be fussy, excitable and eccentric, and not suitable for the role of the doctor on a large sailing vessel with so many passengers. The voyage started in Gravesend on 5 March, proceeded to Queenstown, Ireland, to collect more passengers and departed there on 25 March. The passage was reported in some detail in the *Courier* on Saturday 18 July 1863 as follows:

> *Ship Beejapore, of Liverpool, 1676 tons register, Edward Brabazon Drenning, commander, sailed from Queenstown 3 p.m. of 24th March 1863; experienced light winds up to latitude of Madeira, which was passed on 4th of April, from thence moderate breezes to the equator, which was passed on 17th April; on 16th of April, latitude 1°41 north, longitude 23°38 west, boarded the American ship City of Mobile, 80 days from Calcutta, and bound to London. 17th of April, latitude 00°34 north, longitude 24°04 west, was boarded by a boat from the British ship Sir John Laurence, 79 days from Adelaide, and bound to London, had light S.E. trades, and passed the island of Trinidad on 30th April; from thence had moderate winds from north and N.N.W., and passed the meridian of the Cape of Good Hope in latitude 41°01 S., on*

the 13th May; and from thence had a succession of winds, varying between N.W. and W.S.W., and a great deal of damp weather, and occasionally hail, sleet, and snow; rounded the south end of Van Diemen's Land on the 10th June, and passed Sydney on the 15th June, and from there to Sandy Cape, which place was passed at 4 a.m. on 24th June, had light winds from N. and N.W.; passed Lady Elliot's Island at 8.m. on 24th June and anchored under Cape Capricorn at 8 p.m. to wait for daylight to go into Keppel Bay; 8 a.m. of 25th, light air from S.S.E., got under way and proceeded towards Keppel Bay: 9.30, received a pilot on board, the rocks off Cape Keppel bearing south three-quarters of a mile; 11.50 a.m. anchored off Sea Hill in nine fathoms.

The 250 passengers who embarked at the East India Docks, Gravesend, were a mix of English, Welsh and Scots. Many of the English were from Lancashire, having been displaced when the mills were unable to operate due to cotton exporting stopped because of the American Civil War. As indicated in Chapter 6 when discussing the 1862 voyage of the **Wanata** to Queensland, the Queensland Government was keen to attract immigrants to the colony and had sent emigration agents to Britain and Germany to point out the advantages offered by the new colony. They were offering all full-paying passengers a £18 land order, which could be used in part payment for any land taken up on arrival in the colony, and after a continuous residence of two years in Queensland, another land order for £12 was given. Assisted passengers (i.e. those who paid only half the usual fee of £17 steerage class), were also to receive a land order of £12 at the end of two years' residence. On this passage, the **Beejapore** was carrying both paying and subsidised passengers.

The work of the Roman Catholic Bishop of Queensland, James Quinn, in attracting and supporting emigrants from Ireland following his arrival in the colony in 1860 has been discussed previously, including the establishment of the Queensland Immigration Society and its work in funding the passage of Irish emigrants. Some passengers on the ***Beejapore*** were brought out with assistance from the Society.

The diary of passenger Abijou Good describes the ship as crowded and passengers were packed together:

> …he conducted me below along a narrow gallery and at last he pointed to a small place not much larger than a small pantry and told me that me and my family would be allowed to share that with another man and his family making twelve of us in whole, I went immediately to examine and after being in some time and my eyes had become accustomed to the obscurity of the place, I could distinguish that there were four shelves on which we were to sleep…… one shelf along the side and one along the end I found to be twenty one inches from the floor and the other two was two feet above them, leaving three feet three inches above the top one, the berth clerk told me this was more room than the law allowed but it was allowed by regulations of this ship and that I must occupy one of the bottom shelve and one of the top shelves and the other man must occupy the other two.

> …we got our clothes off and mounted the shelf when we found it was utterly impossible to sit upright so we were compelled to lie down and in a state of sleep and awake we lay till the light of morning began to peep through the ports then I got up and thus passed the first day and night on shipboard.[74]

The first part of the passage from London to Queenstown was slow and disrupted because of the weather. To start the voyage, the ***Beejapore*** was towed down the Thames and into the English Channel. On the day of departure, the weather was fine and bright, but on the following day a choppy headwind arose and soon many passengers, particularly the women and children, were affected by seasickness and the vessel put into Portland Bay for shelter for a couple of days.

---

74 Good, Abijou. Diary of Passage to Queensland on the *Beejapore* 1853. NLA MS513.

The weather improved and the voyage proceeded and the south coasts of Devon were apparently visible through the evening haze. The crossing of Mount's Bay the next day was rough, and it was reported the line from the tug snapped a few times. Finally, the tug moved away and returned up the Channel to London while Captain Drenning headed the ship for Queenstown. On arrival, contrary winds prevented him from entering the harbour for nine or 10 days, but at length the vessel entered the port and was towed to her anchorage off the Queenstown quay.[75]

During the stay in Queenstown, passengers were permitted some shore leave, which meant they would have been exposed to prevailing local illnesses. Meanwhile 450 more passengers, chiefly from Tipperary, were assembled and embarked ready for the passage to Queensland. On the afternoon of the 24 March, 20 days after leaving London, the long voyage to Queensland began, with a tug taking the *Beejapore* in tow to enable her to clear the heads. The Tipperary contingent was chiefly a mix of full-paying and assisted passengers brought out by the Queensland Roman Catholic Prelate, Bishop Quinn, and under the immediate care of Reverend Father Keating during the voyage. The ship now had its full complement of passengers on board. The single men were on the lower deck, the married couples and single girls on the 'tween deck (i.e. the space immediately under the main deck), and the second cabin and intermediate passengers were also on the first deck below the main. Saloon cabins were on the main deck. The single girls were under the care of a matron and for exercising, were restricted to a defined part of the main deck.

When near the equator, the weather was hot and the sea calm. During this part of the voyage the *Beejapore* met the *Sir John Lawrence* from Adelaide, which had been becalmed for six weeks. She took letters for London from the passengers on the *Beejapore*. Later, another vessel, *City of Mobile* from Calcutta, was encountered and letters exchanged.

---

75 Bird, J.T.S. Sixty Years in Queensland Old-Time Migration. Morning Bulletin, Saturday 7 July 1923.

The ***Beejapore*** was becalmed for three days, during which there was some distress for some of the female passengers caused by heat rash (at first thought to be scarlet fever). One of the Irish passengers became tangled in a rope during heavy weather and was tipped overboard. Despite attempts by the crew to rescue him, he drowned. There were two alarms of fire during the voyage and, even though they were dealt with quickly, panic ensued on each occasion. The chief amusements on board were card-playing, dominoes and impromptu singing. After departing Queenstown, it was soon apparent there was insufficient food for the number of people on board and there were problems with the water and no purifier on board.

It wasn't long into the voyage when the first of many deaths occurred. The death was reported in the Good diary as follows:

April 12th

…this morning an Irishman who had been ill ever since he had been on board, died about half past nine. He had numerous family and the ship bell rang with their cry and lamentations. Soon after dinner his body was sewn up in a piece of sail, weights and his bed were then sewn up in his blankets and about four o'clock it was carried by sailors from the hospital to the upper deck. It was placed across the vessel's side on some boards…the priest wished to commence the service but could not be heard for the cries of the bereaved family…in a few minutes the priest's voice ceased, the boards on which the body was laying were raised, the body slipped forward. A splash was heard, the vessel sped on her way and we had one passenger the less…

Diarist Good recorded that the deaths continued:

April 17th

…a child died yesterday, at an early hour in the morning. I was standing on deck about half past seven when I saw a man come

up the hatchway steps carrying a bundle in his arms; he walked to the side of the vessel. I noticed the doctor was behind him with an open book in his hand; they stood about two minutes and then the man threw the bundle overboard...

More children die:

May 20th

This morning a child dies of the measles which is very bad amongst the children and the doctor is of no more use than an old washerwoman. In fact the captain comes round every morning to see who is ill and he seems to know more than the doctor for he gives him directions...

May 28

...two other children died this morning. They were thrown over in short time and no prayers were read for the doctor was not up. He first murders them by neglecting them and then he refuses to read prayers it is too much trouble...

June 6th

...to day death has been very busy amongst us and four children have died and their bodies were thrown over soon after death taking place and no prayers.[76]

There were 667 passengers on board the **Beejapore** for the passage to Queensland. Even with the reduced numbers compared to the first trip to Sydney in 1853, there was considerable overcrowding, disease and discomfort and there were 36 deaths during the passage. The poor conditions on board were reported in the *Rockhampton Bulletin and Central Queensland Advertiser* on Tuesday 30 June 1863.

...we are further told that the medical comforts on board were

---

76 Abijou, Good. Diary of Passage to Queensland on the *Beejapore* 1863. NLA MS513.

utterly insufficient in quantity to meet the natural demands of so large a number of passengers, and that to their deficiency may, in great measure, be attributed the large number of children's deaths occurring during the passage and finally we are assured that the absolute neglect of all sanitary precautions, as manifested by the state of the "Beejapore" on her arrival in Keppel Bay, not only reflects the greatest disgrace on the officers charged with the duty of enforcing cleanliness, but also exposed the passengers to certain decimation had any epidemic attacked them.

The ***Beejapore*** was only the second vessel to go directly to Keppel Bay from England; the ***Eutopia*** had arrived the previous November. Overcrowding was once again a major problem, combined with infectious diseases and a large number of young children. It was this same combination of factors that caused so many deaths on the first passage to Sydney.

The ***Beejapore*** made no further passages to the colonies. She departed Keppel Bay on 16 September 1863 and while on the passage to Callao, Peru, she was lost at sea.

Chapter 10

THE *SHACKAMAXON*

> *To the diggings my father came just ninety years ago*
> *on windjammer "Shackamaxon" depending on the blow*
> *she wallowed oft becalmed, in the gales she flew.*
> *Many months had vanished to see that journey through.*
>
> William Campbell[77]

THE **SHACKAMAXON** WAS built in Philadelphia, USA, in 1851. She was launched on 10 July and put to sea on 2 August. She was a large clipper-style vessel of 1241 tons, 170-foot long, a beam of 37 foot 6 inches and drawing 16 foot 3 inches forward and 17 foot 3 inches aft. Like all the big North American–built vessels of that time, she had two decks beneath the main deck.

It seems she was named after the part of Pennsylvania where William Penn concluded a treaty with the local Indians in 1641. This was reported in *The Adelaide Observer* on 5 February 1853 as follows:

---

77 Taken from the story of Victorian Pioneer William Campbell (1861–1960). His father came to the gold rush in the *Shackamaxon*.

> *The 'Shackamaxon'—This splendid American ship was so called in honour of that beautiful portion of the State of Pennsylvania where William Penn concluded his treaty with the Indians. The ship's embellishments have reference to that event, so memorable in the history of human civilisation; and we are told that some of the ship's massive timbers were felled in one of the adjacent forests, the contemplation of which influenced Penn in designating the State of which he was the founder.*

Soon after launching, the **Shackamaxon** was acclaimed as a beautiful vessel that resembled a frigate due to the painting of false gun ports along its strake. Her figurehead is thought to be a representation of Chief Tamamend of the Lenape tribe. It was said when the **Shackamaxon** was under sail, the figurehead was visible, riding the waves like a gilded billet head (a decorative piece of woodwork that adorns the bow of a ship).

The **Shackamaxon,** although owned by the firm George McHenry & Co., of Philadelphia, was registered in Liverpool and did her first passages between Liverpool and Philadelphia in 1851 under captain William H. West. She was initially used as a packet vessel, making regular trips according to a timetable between the two ports at a cost of 15 guineas per passage. In September 1852 she was the sixth of the large North American–built vessels to be chartered by the Emigration Commission to transport emigrants to the colonies. Her task was to transport almost 800 passengers from Liverpool to Adelaide—these included 696 government emigrants, together with the cabin passengers, officers and ship's crew, making about 780 souls. The master for the voyage was Captain West and the surgeon superintendent was Dr Allison, assisted by Dr Hardy.

The Shackamaxon   159

Ship *Shackamaxon* by Antonio Jacobsen

As with the five other large North American–built ships, it would have taken at least eight days to process and load so many passengers on the **Shackamaxon** as the Birkenhead depot could only accommodate 400 passengers at a time. It appears from later reports the loading of provisions and passengers was undertaken in a hurried manner so they could depart before new legislative provisions came into force. This possibly meant the vessel was not fully equipped for the long passage to the Australian colonies and insufficient care was taken in screening passengers. It seems from later reports the surgeon superintendent, Dr Allison, was rather casual in the processing of the emigrants to determine their fitness for the voyage.

What is recorded about the voyage largely comes from documents and reports developed after the voyage had been completed. They indicate there was much illness during the passage—particularly among the children, who were especially affected by an outbreak of scarlatina. It seems the surgeon superintendent was overwhelmed by the task and his responsibilities and sought assistance from the captain. There was friction between him and the assistant doctor and the structure for supporting passengers and maintaining order broke down. While the ship arrived with the emigrant space clean, unlike some of the other Northern American–built ships, she nevertheless carried many sick passengers and lack of coordination of support decreased their chance of survival. Reports indicate the **Shackamaxon** arrived with 255 children and 401 adult emigrants. There were 19 births during the passage and many deaths. It's difficult to be precise about the exact number of deaths that occurred on the voyage because different numbers are quoted in various reports. The initial press reports mention 57 deaths (six adults and 51 children). The report by the South Australian Immigration Board into the deaths cites a figure of 'sixty deaths which happened at sea' (further details of this investigation are provided below). The Immigration Officer, Dr Duncan, in his quarterly report (also see below) provides a figure of 64, of which 54 were children under seven years of age. To further confuse the issue, on 22 January the *Adelaide Observer* included in a report on the deaths the name of each adult and child who died, including their age and place of origin. The numbers in that report were six adults and 48 children—a total of 54. The Emigration Commission cites a different figure to all these in responding to queries from the Colonial Office as follows:

> The 'Shackamaxon' was the last of the large ships which the peculiar circumstances of last year compelled us to take up. She sailed from Liverpool on 4th of October, having on board 696 emigrants, equal to 533 statute adults; the number of births on the voyage was 19, making a total of 715 souls; the total number of deaths was 65, equal to about 9 per cent, but of these 15 were infants, 34 were three years of age, or under; nine were from four to 14 inclusive, and only seven were above 14. The principal cause of death was scarlatina, which prevailed during the whole voyage, and which would appear from the surgeon's journal to have been in the ship before she sailed.[78]

---

78 T.W.C. Murdock and F. Rogers to H. Melville, enclosure 1 in no. 6, 23 August 1853, 'Correspondence relating to emigration to the Australian colonies', BPP 1854 vol. XLVI, 33.

The vessel was not placed in quarantine, even though there were still some sick people (possibly children) on board when the **Shackamaxon** arrived and there is one report that states a child died on the first night in port. The entry to port was delayed because of the size of the vessel and she was made to wait until there was enough water to clear the bar.

The initial reports of the arrival of the **Shackamaxon** were incredibly positive because they focused on her size and beauty. People went to Port Adelaide to look at her because she was the largest vessel to visit the port up to that time. As an example, the *Adelaide News* published the following account on 1 April 1953 as a reflection 100 years on from her arrival in Adelaide. It is a conversation between Dr Duncan (port medical officer) and the pilot as they approached the **Shackamaxon**:

From his seat in the stern, Dr. Duncan, the port medical officer, expressed his appreciation of the fine ship the pilot boat was approaching over the dancing morning waves.

'A magnificent vessel,' he said to the pilot. 'I doubt if I have seen a lovelier.' 'A regular beauty.' the pilot agreed 'It's an honour to Adelaide to have her moored at the Port.' The Shackamaxon deserved their praise. A United States built ship, of 1,200 tons, she had been launched in 1851 at Philadelphia. Since then, she had been the admiration of every port where she had anchored. Her slender, frigate-like lines beheld her three solid decks and the mainmast 30 in. in diameter. This was her first visit to Adelaide. Chartered by the British Government, she had sailed from Liverpool on October 4, 1852, with 696 migrants on board. 'Sullen lot fortunate people', Dr. Duncan reflected, as the pilot boat came alongside the Jacob's ladder. To be assisted out to South Australia and to travel in such a ship was luck indeed. He followed the pilot up the ship's side and was pleased to note that the Shackamaxon was just as beautiful close up as she was from a distance-decks scrubbed, ropes coiled, and sails furled as carefully as a woman folds her best dress.

Unfortunately, despite the pristine condition of the vessel, the passage had been a nightmare for some individuals and families. There were many families mourning the loss of a child or children, mainly the victims of scarlatina. The story of the illness and death that was part of the voyage is contained in the following report from the *South Australian Register* of 20 January 1853:

THE EMIGRANT SHIP 'SHACKAMAXON.'

The satisfaction caused by the first announcement of this arrival was soon followed by feelings of deep regret when it was ascertained that a considerable number of deaths had occurred on the passage.

The beautiful ship Shackamaxon, 2500 tons, left Liverpool on the 4th of October, having on board 696 Government emigrants; the cabin passengers, officers, and ship's crew making a total of about 780 souls. We have the authority of the Liverpool Standard for the statement that the Shackamaxon and three other large ships bound to the Australian colonies were sent to sea sooner than their charterers would have desired, and probably at some inconvenience to them, owing to the circumstance that, under the new Emigration Act, coming into operation in October, their fittings, &c, might have had to be remodelled to comply with its requirements if they had remained longer in port. We fear that this hurry to get away may have contributed in some measure to the sad amount of mortality which all must deplore. We have now before us lists of 57 deaths and 19 births; but as we recognise the same names in both lists, the deaths may include several of the infants, and we forbear to publish either until we can distinguish the deaths of very young children from those which have occurred among the passengers of riper years. The names of the many hundreds who have arrived will be found in our Shipping Intelligence column. It will doubtless have been observed by many of our readers that on board several of the very large emigrant ships which have arrived latterly at Melbourne, the mortality has been very considerable; and such a succession of evil tidings will doubtless lead to serious inquiry by H.M. Commissioners in England as to the propriety and expediency of sending so large a number of families and individuals in one ship. Here the Government and the Immigration Agent have a special duty to perform in the case of the Shackamaxon, and we have no doubt that the inquiries and examinations of Dr. Duncan will be followed by a luminous report and the requisite publicity.

Whilst the ship remained in the Mersey, her beauty of proportion and frigate-like appearance attracted universal admiration; but we fear that there may have been insufficient ventilation, or an incompleteness in the arrangements and special supplies necessary for the well-being of an unusually large body of emigrants undertaking so long a voyage. The duration of passages from England to Australia by sailing vessels having been astonishingly lessened by the application of science, experience, and the employment of superior vessels, we cannot be reconciled to such painful disparagements as those which have recently occurred. In the case of the Fairfield, which arrived here from Liverpool with emigrants in 1849, after a voyage of six months, the only death was that of an infant born on board; and in the case of the Trusty from Gravesend, which arrived here in 1838, there were only two deaths, although four births occurred, during a long passage of 24 weeks.

Initially, Dr Duncan had reported the ship was clean and orderly and he felt that was because of the efforts of the surgeon superintendent, Dr Allison, and that Dr Allison could not be held responsible for the deaths. However, over 100 of the passengers petitioned the lieutenant governor, demanding an investigation into the incompetence of Dr Allison. As a result, the Immigration Board was convened to investigate the cause of so many deaths on the voyage to Adelaide and to report to the lieutenant governor, Sir Henry Edward Fox Young.

Charges of neglect and inappropriate conduct were made against the surgeon superintendent, the assistant doctor, the matron and the religious instructor. Dr Allison had eight charges made against him, but many were minor or trivial and were dismissed by the Board. The assistant surgeon, Dr Hardy, had no specific charges made against him but his conduct and the manner in which he performed his duties was investigated by the Board. The religious instructor, James Fawsett, had 15 charges made against him, most of which were also minor or trivial. The Board did find, however, there was evidence to support the charge of drunkenness and did not approve 'of a person in the position of religious instructor dancing on deck with emigrant girls placed under his religious superintendence'. The matron, Elizabeth Cooper, had 15 charges laid against her, largely about not fulfilling her role as protector, guardian and supervisor of the single women as set out in the rules provided by the emigration commissioners. It's interesting that James Fawsett and Elizabeth Cooper were married by the captain during the passage (as practiced on American vessels) but were married again by the deputy-registrar in Adelaide soon after arrival. The Board found most of the charges were proven. It also found the problems on the voyage were exacerbated by the inability of the surgeon superintendent to maintain control of the assistant surgeon, religious instructor and matron who ignored his authority and undermined his position with the crew and passengers.

The immigration agent's report for the quarter ended 31 March, was published in the *Government Gazette* on Thursday 14 April and then reproduced in full in the *Adelaide Times* on Saturday 16 April 1853. An extract from that report is reproduced below:

> *In the Shackamaxon, while at sea and in port, before final disembarkation, sixty-four deaths occurred amongst the emigrants of these deaths, fifty-four were of children, under seven years of age.*
>
> *The greater number of the deaths resulted from the consequences of*

scarlatina, which prevailed during the whole voyage. There were many cases of whooping-cough and dysentery. On arrival, the ship was in excellent order, and the persons and bedding of the emigrants were clean and tidy.

In consequence of the very many serious charges having been brought against the Surgeon Superintendent, an Immigration Board was called together, to investigate all the circumstances connected with the discipline, general management, and medical treatment of the emigrants. This Board, after a long and patient investigation, sent in a Special Report to His Excellency the Lieutenant Governor. The Report, having gone minutely into detail, states in conclusion:—'The Board regret to be obliged to say, that four of the persons appointed by the Commissioners—the Surgeon-Superintendent, the Assistant-Surgeon, the Religious Instructor, and the Matron-not one performed, with the least approach to efficiency, the responsible duties with which they were intrusted and in another place "That the decision and energy of Captain West were, in a great measure, the means of averting consequences which, might have been most disastrous." In consequence of this Report, His Excellency the Lieutenant-Governor was pleased to order that the payment of all gratuities to the officers appointed by the Commissioners should be stopped.

I have the honour to be, Sir, your obedient servant,

H. DUNCAN, M.D.,

Immigration Agent.

The enquiry had been conducted in secrecy and received only passing references in the press during the weeks that it took to conduct it. The public appeared disinterested in the investigation by the Board, but they were certainly interested in the vessel. There were a few letters to the newspapers about the matter, but there was little protest over the findings of the Board except from James Fawsett, the religious instructor. He claimed the inquiry had been grossly unfair and he had been found guilty on the evidence of one witness, while four he had produced in his own defence were not even examined. Although there were only a small number of comments made in the newspapers, some were along the lines that the four charged were scapegoats for the large number of problems that led to sickness, the breakdown of discipline, the lack of support arrangements and to the deaths on the **Shackamaxon**. The loss of the gratuities by all four would have been difficult to accept, particularly for Dr Allison, as the chief medical officer, as this could have meant the loss of over £300 (a substantial amount in 1853).

Captain West was highly regarded by the passengers and the Immigration Board agreed he had performed his duties exceptionally well on the passage from Liverpool to Adelaide. Several testimonials to Captain West appeared in the Adelaide newspapers during January, including one signed by over 200 passengers. While in port, the **Shackamaxon** attracted a constant stream of visitors and on February 23 the captain gave an elaborate luncheon, which was attended by the lieutenant governor, the bishop of Adelaide, the surveyor-general, and other 'leading' citizens. In March, advertisements appeared in the newspapers relating to the return passage, such as the one below in the *Adelaide Times* on Thursday 31 March 1853:

FOR LIVERPOOL VIA SWANSEA.

To sail positively on the 3rd April.

This splendid new fast-sailing A1 United States ship SHACKAMAXON,

1,500 tons, Wm. Henry West, commander, will be despatched for the above ports on 3rd April. In order to effect a material saving to shippers of Gold and Wool, as regards the Insurance, she

guarantees not to take more than two-thirds her register tonnage of dead weight; the whole of which is engaged. Wool will lie taken on board without pressing.

Her accommodations for cabin and intermediate passengers are magnificent. Parties desirous of a comfortable and speedy voyage to England are requested to inspect this fine vessel.

This vessel is provided with Phillips' Patent Fire Annihilator and carries an experienced Surgeon.

For rates of passage, or freight on Gold and Wool, apply to Captain West on board; or to

JOSEPH STILLING & CO, Adelaide; or JOHN NEWMAN, Port. Captain West will attend at the office of the undersigned on Mondays, Wednesdays, and Fridays, from 10 to 12 o'clock, for the purpose of signing bills of lading.

JOSEPH STILLING & CO. March 15th, 1853.

When the ship sailed on 4 April, the *Register* printed a lengthy eulogy on its incomparable beauty and the boundless hospitality of its officers. Its departure was not marred by any tactless press references to the unfortunate voyage out. Nor did the memory affect the passenger list for the 'cream' of Adelaide society returned to England, cabin class, on what must have been the 1853 equivalent of a luxury cruise. The bishop of Adelaide, with his wife and six children, was a passenger. In the ship's holds were 800 tons of rich copper ore and wool in place of steerage-class emigrants and in the purser's strong box 15,000 ounces of gold. In order to make room for cargo for the return voyage, the two decks below the main deck were stripped of all the fittings needed to accommodate the steerage immigrants on the passage to Adelaide. As was common practice with vessels returning with cargo, the fittings and excess goods were auctioned. In the case of the **Shackamaxon** this occurred soon after arrival. The notice of auction appeared in the *South Australian Register* Tuesday 1 February 1853:

> MONDAY. *February 7th.* SURPLUS STORES AND FIT-TINGS OF THE UNITED STATES SHIP 'SHACKA-MAXON.' TO GROCERS, STOREKEEPERS, SHIPMAS-TERS, AND OTHERS. SOLOMON & CO. *are instructed to sell by public auction, on board the splendid frigate-built ship Shackamaxon, on Monday, February 7th, at 12 o'clock — The whole of her very superior* SURPLUS STORES, FITTINGS, *&c., consisting of all the requisites usually found in an emigrant ship, and all of the very best quality and large quantities, amongst which will be found-Bottled Beer, Wines of first-rate description, Tea, Loaf and Fine Sugar, Raisins, Currants, Peas, Rice, Sago, Arrowroot, Barley, Tapioca, Spirits, Vinegar, Lime Juice, Pickles, Mess Beef, Mess Pork, Soap, Buckets and Mess Kits, Tin Ware and Brushes, Birch Brooms, Water Casks and an immense variety of sundries.* AFTER WHICH, *the very superior Fittings of this fine ship, put up to accommodate the large number of 700 passengers.*

Ship *Shackamaxon* lithograph by C.P. Williams

When the ***Shackamaxon*** departed, it left behind the families of those that had died on the passage out. They were left with the memories of the horrors associated with the passage to Adelaide. For the parents of the dead children, those memories would have included the dreadful sight of little bodies wrapped in canvas being cast into the sea. Like the other large two-decker vessels, the ***Shackamaxon*** was grossly overcrowded on that voyage, which meant the rapid spread of infectious disease was inevitable. It's evident an infectious disease was present at the commencement of the voyage and it appears at least in the first part of the passage the need for cleanliness may have been ignored. In its General Summary, the Board commented:

> …*it is on record in the medical journal of the ship that several cases of scarlet fever were under treatment before the ship sailed from Liverpool, though according to the regulations of the Commissioners it is to be presumed that the Surgeon Superintendent gave a certificate to the pilot on leaving the vessel that no infectious disorder existed.*
>
> *The Board cannot but attribute the contagion produced by the cases of scarlet fever then under treatment to the great subsequent prevalence of the disease and the large number of deaths which occurred.*
>
> …*whether from inability or negligence it is difficult to decide, but the regulations made by the Commissioners for cleaning the ship were not put in force till she had been four weeks at sea, and the dirt had accumulated to an alarming extent before the Surgeon Superintendent seems to have moved in the matter.* [79]

Despite the problems with the ***Shackamaxon***'s first passage to the colonies, she made further voyages there, including as an emigration vessel under charter to the Emigration Commission. While she did

---

79 Immigration Board Report 'Shackamaxon' to His Excellency Sir H. Young, Lieutenant Governor of South Australia. 2 March 1853. State Library of South Australia GRG 24/78.

not return to Adelaide, there are records of visits she made to Victoria, New South Wales and Queensland. Like many American-built ships at that time, she was admired and highly valued in the market. At an auction on 7 December 1854, she was sold for £28,000.

The first voyage to Melbourne was announced in the *Age* on Friday 5 October 1855:

> PORT PHILLIP HEADS. ARRIVED. *October 4— Shackamaxon, ship, 1376 tons, from Liverpool 21st June. General cargo. 100 passengers, Bright Brothers and Co., agents.*

There are no details of the passengers, the voyage, or of the state of the ship on arrival. With only 100 passengers, there would have been much more space per person and hence a much more comfortable passage than on the one to Adelaide. It's also probably safe to assume the second deck was only used for transporting the 'general cargo'.

The next record is of a voyage to Queensland in 1859. She departed Birkenhead in August under contract to the Emigration Commission at a price of £14 14 s 0d per head. The arrival and disembarkation by steamer was reported in the *Moreton Bay Courier* on Saturday 26 November 1859:

> LOCAL INTELLIGENCE.
>
> NEWLY ARRIVED IMMIGRANTS. *—The steamer Breadalbane brought up the immigrants from the " Shackamaxon" yesterday. With the exception of one or two, all are in excellent health, and speak in the highest terms of the kindness and attention of Capt. Teulon, and Dr. Graham, the latter of whom has twice before visited this port in the same capacity. A birth occurred yesterday morning, before the passengers left the ship, and the mother and her little one were both carefully transferred from the vessel to the steamer. The immigrants will be for hire on Monday next, and the particulars of the different callings are given in our advertising*

columns. In mentioning this, we feel bound to refer to the obstinate violation of rule by many persons, who, in spite of all that may be said to them, persevere in entering the depot, and engaging servants previous to the time advertised. It is unfair to the public, and especially to those residing at a distance, for any individual to tamper with the immigrants prior to the advertised day, and we know that a stringent system of exclusion is maintained in Sydney and elsewhere.

This was also a smooth passage in terms of passenger health and welfare. It appears some passengers on the voyage came out under a type of bounty arrangement as indentured workers. They were apparently recruited by a labour agent acting on behalf of rural employers. There was a lengthy article in the *Moreton Bay Courier* on Wednesday 30 November, very critical of the terms of the agreements the emigrants had signed and of the propriety of the financial arrangements. It stated, in part:

THE arrival of the Shackamaxon has led to the exposure of a novel species of immigration – a system which, having private ends in view, is being carried out at the expense of the public. It seems that a large proportion of the adult immigrants by this vessel have come out under suspicious agreements entered into by them in London. Mr. J. H. SCOTT DUBBIN being the party by whom they were engaged, and he being the agent of the various squatters to whom they are indented.

The **Shackamaxon** was reported to have cleared the bar and departed from the Bay and from Queensland on Saturday 31 December 1859.

The **Shackamaxon** next appeared in Australian waters on a passage to Melbourne in 1861, having departed Liverpool on 7 November 1860. For this voyage she had again been engaged by the Emigration Commission to bring immigrants to Victoria. The emigrants arrived in good health and their number was about the number that would have been transported on a medium-sized one-deck vessel of the type that brought most emigrants to the colonies in the nineteenth century. In addition to carrying about half the number of passengers that were transported to Adelaide in 1853, the number of children on the voyage was only a fraction of the some 250 that were on the passage to Adelaide. There were also positive comments in the press about Dr Jolley, the surgeon superintendent, the good work that he did on the passage in taking care of the welfare of passengers and the fact that it was his tenth passage in the service of the emigration commissioners. The arrival was reported in the *Argus* on Thursday 31 January as follows:

SHIPPING INTELLIGENCE. ARRIVED. - JAN, 29.

Shackamaxon, ship, 989 tons, John B. Teulon, from Liverpool 8th November, with 345 Government immigrants. Dr. Jolley, surgeon superintendent. De Pass Brothers, agents.

The ship Shackamaxon arrived in Hobson's Bay late on Tuesday evening. She brings a large number of Government immigrants. One casualty occurred; a man being accidentally killed. The immigrants are in good health, and the vessel is thoroughly clean.

The following is the classification of the immigrants which arrived by the ship Shackamaxon:-- Married couples, 28; single women, 255; single men 3; children under 14 years, 23; infants 9.

In the same issue of the *Age*, it was reported the hiring of the immigrants who had arrived in the **Shackamaxon** had been postponed until the following Saturday, 2 February, because of the inclemency of the weather and the inability to land.

Port Phillip 1853 by Thomas Kelly
(State Library of Victoria)

She was back in Melbourne in 1862, having again transported emigrants for the Emigration Commission. The *Argus* reported the docking on Thursday 20 March 1862 as follows:

> *The Ship Shackamaxon, with her Government Immigrants on board, was towed alongside the Government Railway Pier, Williamtown, yesterday morning. Her passengers were forwarded to Melbourne by special train.*

The *Age* carried the following advertisement on Saturday 29 March 1862:

> *BLACK BALL & EAGLE LINES OF PACKETS*
> *FOR POINT DE GALLE*
> *The celebrated clipper ship;*
> *SHACKAMAXON*

> *Teulon master, will be despatched on 3rd April. For passage apply to:*
> BRIGHT BROS. and CO. Agents.

In 1863 the **Shackamaxon** transported emigrants to Sydney again under charter for the Emigration Commission. The *Freeman's Journal* reported on Saturday 18 July 1863 her departure from Liverpool:

> *The Shackamaxon, 989 tons, belonging to, Messrs Joseph Heap and Sons, of Liverpool, sailed from Birkenhead, on May 12, for Sydney, New South Wales, with 386 Government emigrants, comprising 42 married couples, 109 single men, 99 single women, and 94 children, equal to 333 statute adults, under the care of Thomas Slater, Esq., surgeon superintendent assisted by Miss Barker, matron.*

Having departed Liverpool on 12 May, she didn't arrive until 3 September as there was a problem with illness and she was placed in quarantine on arrival. This may have been a temporary requirement until the situation was assessed. Although the number of emigrants was small compared to the first passage and about the same size as many single-deck vessels would transport, the number of children was reasonably high, making up almost 25 per cent of the passengers. On about 12 September a launch transported some 60 emigrants from the **Shackamaxon** to Circular Quay Wharf; presumably the remaining passengers were still in quarantine. It seems she departed Sydney on Wednesday 23 December 1863. A notice in the *Empire* (Sydney) on 21 December read:

SHIP SHACKAMAXON

Passengers are requested to be on board on TUESDAY as the ship will sail at daylight on WEDNESDAY.

There is no record of any further passages to the Australian colonies.

It's interesting that the Merseyside Maritime Museum in Liverpool has a recreation of the **Shackamaxon** in the Emigrants to a New World Gallery. This gallery takes visitors back to Liverpool in 1854, where a recreation of a street scene leads down to the docks to the emigrant ship **Shackamaxon.** Going on board this ship and 'seeing the lanterns sway and the ship creak is the strongest image taken away from the museum by the visitor'. A focus in the recreated ship is the environment where steerage-class passengers made their journey.

The **Shackamaxon** was still on the Liverpool Register of Shipping (Official Ship Number 1293) at 29 June 1864. However, there is a handwritten annotation on the registration page for the **Shackamaxon** as follows:

> *Custom House, Liverpool Cancelled 3 Dec 1979. Used as a hulk at Bonny, West Coast of Africa as per letter from the Secretary to the British African Steam Navigation Co, Agents to the Registered owner (deceased) dated 2nd Dec 1879. Registry closed 3 Dec 1879.*[80]

Thus, it seems she ended her days as a hulk on the West Coast of Africa and her entry in the registry was closed on 3 December 1879. Bonny is a town and Atlantic port in southern Nigeria. It lies along the Bonny River (an eastern distributary of the Niger River) 6 miles upstream from the Bight of Biafra. A traditional trading centre (fish, salt, palm oil and palm kernels), it was the capital of the fifteenth-to-nineteenth-century kingdom of Bonny. It's interesting to note Liverpool, where the Shackamaxon was registered, was a key port in the British slave trade, and Bonny, where she ended her sailing life, was one of the largest slave-exporting depots of West Africa during the eighteenth and early nineteenth centuries. It's a little sad for a ship to end her life as a hulk, as this meant the hull structure was too old and weak to

---

80 Copy of page from register provided by the Assistant Curator, Maritime Archives & Library, Merseyside Maritime Museum.

withstand the stresses of sailing. As a hulk she would have still been afloat, but all the rigging and internal equipment would have been removed and she would no longer have been recognisable as a fine nineteenth-century ship or admired for her 'beauty of appearance'.

Chapter 11

CONCLUSION

And they in hammocks sewed, and ranged to lee,
With weight attached of gun-shot and of lead,
Were cast, lamented, in the briny sea -
Their mortal grave.

The Black Death, A Poem of the Sea. M.J.Home

THESE SIX LARGE double-decked vessels had been engaged by the Emigration Commissioners so they could meet the urgent and pressing demands of the colonies for immigrants to be transported and meet local demands for labour. This demand was mainly caused by workers leaving for the goldfields. There was a sense of desperation in the call for labour—particularly by New South Wales, Victoria and South Australia—because of the impact on the rural industries that had been so important to the wealth of the colonies. Using the large double-deck vessels was seen as a way to move large numbers of people to the colonies quickly as these vessels were able to reach their destination much more rapidly than the usual emigration vessels, such as the traditional square-rigged ships. Let's not forget these large North American–vessels were also impressive-looking ships and appeared to be spacious. For example, a report in the *South Australian Register* on 20 January 1853 included the following comment about the **Shackamaxon**:

> *Whilst the ship remained in the Mersey, her beauty of proportion and frigate-like appearance attracted universal admiration…*

Much to the horror of the Emigration Commissioners and the colonial authorities, there were many deaths during the passages on these vessels and sometimes deaths also occurred during quarantine after their arrival. There were several investigations and official enquiries. Four of the vessels had taken emigrants from Liverpool to Victoria and the combined death at sea and during quarantine was 356 souls.[81] The Annual Report of the Victorian Immigration Agent, Edward Grimes, prepared for the Victorian Colonial Secretary, dated 9 June 1853, attributes the disaster of this and a number of other ships to gross overcrowding. The following are excerpts from that report:

> *2. The vast and hitherto unprecedented influx of population to this colony during the latter part of the year 1852, and which has continued steadily to increase up to the present date, owing to the discovery and rapid developments of the gold-fields of Victoria, renders the subject which I am now called upon to consider, one of more than ordinary importance; while the inadequacy of the accommodation afforded by this city to furnish even temporary shelter to the myriads now landing daily on our shores, has become a matter of serious and increasing anxiety…*
>
> *5. The first return which I have to bring under your Excellency's notice is Return No. 4, which contains particulars of the ships chartered by Her Majesty's Colonial Land and Emigration Commissioners for the conveyance of Immigrants to Victoria, giving the various details connected therewith.*

---

[81] Annual Report of the Immigration Officer 1853 p. 3. Parliament of Victoria GP V 1853/54 no. A1.

From this return it will be seen that the impulse given by the gold discovery to assisted immigration has been very great, no less than forty-two ships, conveying in all 15,477 souls, having cast anchor in our waters in 1852. Of these immigrants 5007 were adult males, and 5345 adult females, the remaining 5125 being children.

I regret to state that the number of deaths which has occurred on the voyage amounted to 840, forming a large percentage on the whole. This result I attribute, in a great measure, to the practice recently adopted of embarking large numbers of from six to eight hundred people on board two-decked ships, as it will be seen in only four ships, Bourneuf, Marco Polo, Wanata and Ticonderoga, the united deaths amounted to no less than 356.

It is gratifying to remark, however, that during the current year, and since Her Majesty's Colonial Land and Emigration Commissioners have abandoned this pernicious system, and refrained from sending out more than 350 souls in vessels of moderate size, the per-centage of mortality has very much decreased…

…The number of assisted immigrants landed at the several ports was as follows:

	Souls	Statute Adults
Melbourne	7877	6398
Geelong	5258	4302
Portland	2342	1889
Total	15,477	12,590

The number of births which occurred on board the various ships was 270, of which 148 were males, and 122 females.

It was found necessary to place four of these ships, viz., the

> *Bourneuf, Wanata, Chance,* and *Ticonderoga*, in quarantine, the principal diseases being scarlet fever, typhus fever, and measles.
>
> *Of the forty-eight surgeons superintendent and assistant surgeons, it was found necessary to withhold the usual gratuity or certificate from two only, a fact which speaks well for the care bestowed in the selection of those officers.*
>
> *This return will show that in the six months ending 31st December, 1852, no fewer than thirty-three vessels containing 12,956 souls arrived; whereas, in the corresponding six months of 1851, the number of ships was seven, and the number of passengers 1987…*
>
> *8. The great disproportion which appears in the number of the Scotch sent out may possibly be attributed to the destitution existing in the Highlands and islands of Scotland, a subject to which I shall have occasion hereinafter more particularly to advert…*[82]

Grimes' annual report had in part been informed by the earlier reports of the individual investigations undertaken in Victoria into mortality on board the emigrant ships **Bourneuf, Wanata, Marco Polo** and **Ticonderoga**, which had been forwarded to the Emigration Commissioners. In his covering letter to the Secretary of State for the Colonies, dated 21 October 1852, La Trobe commented:

> *I consider it my duty to take the earlier opportunity of bringing under your notice the very serious objections which may be raised against chartering of vessels of great burthen for the transport of large bodies of emigrants to this colony.*
>
> *2. With this view, I beg leave to transmit, and recommend to immediate consideration, a copy of a report which I have directed the immigration agent to draw up on this subject, distinctly stating the grounds upon which the objections gathered from the experiments hitherto made may be based; and further copies of the reports of the*

---

82 Ibid pp. 3–4.

Board of Immigration upon the 'Marco Polo', the 'Wanata' and the 'Bourneuf', respectively, all of which remark upon various points in connexion with this subject, to which the attention of Her Majesty's Government should be at once directed.[83]

The report on the **Ticonderoga** was subsequently forwarded by Herman Merivale, undersecretary of the Colonial Office, to the commissioners at the direction of the Duke of Newcastle, Secretary of State for War and the Colonies, with the comment:

His Grace desires me to request that you will cause an immediate and searching inquiry to be made into all the circumstances of various and distressing cases of mortality which have occurred on board so many emigrant ships.[84]

The horror expressed by the Emigration Commission at the number of deaths on these large vessels led, in part, to a defensive response. It's clear the Commission was concerned about its reputation and safety record as it concluded its report with the following statement:

We may be permitted to point out that the present instances are the first of any large mortality in ships chartered by this Board. On the contrary, we have sent out to the Australian colonies, between the beginning of 1847 and the end of 1851, no less than 235 ships, carrying 61,696 emigrants, with an average mortality of 1.81 per cent. And as regards the future, we hope and believe that in the absence of any uncontrollable cause of disease, the steps which we have taken will avail to restore to our ships that healthy character, for which, until last year, we had reason to be thankful.[85]

---

83   C. J Latrobe to Emigration Commission 21 October 1852. House of Commons Parliamentary papers, Encl in No. 1 (no. 142).

84   Merivale to Emigration Commissioners 1 February 1853. House of Commons Parliamentary papers, No. 2 .

85   Emigration Commission to Merivale, 11 February 1853 in 'Papers relative to emigration to the Australian colonies' No.15. 1852–53 (1627), LXVIII, 188.

Prior to receiving the direction to prepare a report on the high mortality on these ships, the commissioners had been busy investigating the causes and had sought reports from agencies, particularly from the Government Immigration Office in Liverpool. The reports requested by the Commission included the surveys undertaken on each of the vessels, provisioning, medical supplies, standard of fit-out and if the number of statute adults had exceeded the number approved for each vessel. Having already received this information, the Commission was able to respond quickly on 11 February 1853 with a lengthy report to Merivale. Their report included the following comments:

> *As regards to adults, we see no reason to distrust the judgement which we had thus formed. The adult mortality on board the 'Wanata' is not extraordinary, and in the 'Bourneuf' and 'Marco Polo' it is very small. But on the children, it is evident that the effect has been very injurious in propagating and giving virulence to diseases which medical treatment might otherwise have kept under. Deeply as we regard this result, we trust it will be believed that the course which we adopted did not proceed from any neglect of or indifference to the welfare of our emigrants, but from the impossibility of refusing, in so extraordinary an emigration as that of last year, to relax the rules which experience had shown to be safe but had not shown to be indispensable.*

> *And this appears a proper place for pointing out that important causes of mortality exist in respect of a Government emigration, from which private ships are comparatively exempt. In private ships the passengers are generally of a class far less susceptible to diseases than the Irish and Highland labourers who form a large part of an assisted emigration…and what is still more important… are unencumbered by families of small children. In our ships the children below four years of age have lately formed from 12 to 18 per cent of the whole emigration.*

> *On the first information which reached us of the mortality in our ships, and before receiving either of the letters under reply, we had already advertised our intention to employ no two-decked vessels in the emigration service and had determined on a more stringent rule with regard to children. We shall hereafter accept no families in which there are more than two children under seven, or more than three under 10; and the desire to emigrate to Australia is now so strong, that we can make the change without any risk of not filling our ships. We shall also take measures so to allot our emigrants, as to reduce as much as possible the proportion of children shipped in vessels of more than 1,000 tons burden.*
>
> *It is proper to inform the Duke of Newcastle, that of 98 ships engaged by us during the last year, only 10 have carried more than 500, and eight (of which these are four) more than 600 persons.*[86]

Having reported in February 1853, the Commission was nevertheless aware of a problem with another large vessel that had departed Scotland in December 1852, but had been diverted to Ireland because of an outbreak of smallpox. This was not a North American–built vessel but rather an old 74-gun ship of the Royal Navy line, the **HMS Hercules**, built in 1815. The Emigration Commission had identified the **Hercules** as a vessel that could transport many emigrants from the Western Highlands and Islands of Scotland to Victoria and South Australia. The Commission was clearly pleased with the arrangements that it had negotiated relating to the fit-out and provisioning on the vessel. In a letter dated 22 November 1852 to the South Australian Colonial Secretary, the Secretary to the Commission, S. Walcott, commented:

> *I am directed by the Colonial Land and Emigration Commissioners to acquaint you for the information of the Lieut.-Governor, that Her -Majesty's ship Hercules has been placed at the disposal of this Board for the conveyance to South Australia and Victoria, of*

---

86 Ibid.

> about 800 Scotch emigrants selected by the Highland and Island Emigration Society. The condition on which the ship was assigned for this service was that she should be fitted and provisioned by the Commissioners at the expense of the Colonial Fund. This has accordingly been done by public tender, at a cost which will probably not exceed £4 10s per statute adult; thus effecting a great saving of passage money on the emigrants sent out in this vessel, as the current rates paid at present by the Commissioner in ordinary ships average upwards of fifteen guineas per statute adult.

After considerable planning and a special fit-out, the **Hercules** moved from the Thames to Campbeltown, Scotland, where 747 emigrants selected by the Highland & Island Emigration Society were embarked. The selected emigrants were made up of 406 selected for South Australia and 341 for Victoria and included 248 children, 19 of whom were under one year.[87] The voyage, which commenced on 26 December 1852, proved disastrous, beginning almost immediately with a horrific storm, during which the ship sought refuge at Rothesay. Damage was caused by the storm, but the vessel was able to recommence the passage in early January 1853. Soon after their second departure, outbreaks of smallpox and later typhus were discovered, necessitating a three-month quarantine at Queenstown, County Cork. Those who were sick on arrival were taken, after some negotiation, to the naval hospital at Hawlbowline Island. While the ship lay in harbour, disease continued to spread among the remaining passengers. Eventually all passengers were moved off the vessel and she was fumigated and internally whitewashed. Fifty-six emigrants and the surgeon died, 17 orphaned children were returned home and many of the healthy passengers were assigned to other ships, families being broken up in the process. When the **Hercules** departed Ireland on 14 April, she had on board only 381 emigrants (approximately half the original number). After a voyage of 104 days, she arrived (via the Cape) at the Light Boat, Port Adelaide on 26 July, carrying 194 emigrants for South Australia. Following an overnight stay, she departed for Victoria on 27

---

87 Guide to the Records of the Highland and Islands Emigration Society 1852–67. NLA MS 156.

July. The vessel arrived in Victoria on 1 August 1853 with the remaining emigrants. Eight people died on the passage from Queenstown to Victoria. The deaths that occurred while the vessel was in quarantine in Ireland were not recorded as voyage deaths but were registered as deaths in the United Kingdom. This was another instance of an unfortunate mix of many passengers, including a high proportion of children, in a crowded vessel together with an outbreak of one or more of the contagious diseases of the nineteenth century.

HMS Hercules **Leaving Campbeltown Harbour, Scotland**
(*Illustrated London News*, Saturday 15 January 1853)

The many deaths, investigations and enquiries, and the considerable negative publicity branded the two-deck ships as death ships. You might imagine this would have damaged their reputation to the extent they would have been considered as unsafe to use to transport emigrants and possibly as carriers of paying passengers. The Emigration Commissioners in fact quickly announced they would not consider using double-deck vessels again for the transport of emigrants to the colonies. However, some of these vessels continued to transport people to the colonies and the **Marco Polo**, **Wanata** and **Shackamaxon** were again commissioned by the Emigration Commission (under amended conditions).

The reports the Emigration Commission received—and that assisted it to form its views and conclusion— dismissed the claims made about the inadequacy of the vessels to carry so many passengers; the inadequacy of food and medical supplies; the fit-out of the vessels; and problems with the Birkenhead depot and hasty departures. The reports on these complaints stated all the vessels had been measured and it had been determined the space provided was appropriate for the number that embarked on each vessel. The dates of embarkation and departure were provided for each vessel and the impression was there was adequate time for all processes to be followed and, hence, there was no undue haste with vessel departure. With regard to impure water, it was stated all the casks taken onboard were new, carefully checked and filled with water 'noted for its purity'. The food and medical supplies were provided in the quantities requested in the contract for the number of statute adults to be transported. Complaints about poor fittings and equipment were also dismissed. For example, the complaints about the dampness and smells from leaky water closets were dismissed on the basis they were of the best design and the problem was people didn't know how to use them and so water was left running.

As I indicated above, despite the definite statements by the Emigration Commission it would no longer use two-decked vessels for the emigrants it was responsible for moving to Australia, it later commissioned three vessels on more than one occasion. However, it does appear the Commission later viewed these vessels as single-deck passenger vessels with an extra deck for cargo. In using these vessels, it reapplied the old rules relating to number and ages of children and reduced the total number of emigrants per vessel. The experience using this formula appears to have been successful in avoiding large numbers of deaths. As a further example of this approach, another large North American vessel, the **Dirigo**, built in 1854 in New Brunswick, was chartered in that year to take 484 passengers to Adelaide. She departed Liverpool on 8 August and arrived at Port Adelaide on 21 November 1854. It seems, unlike the **Shackamaxon** in January 1853, the ***Dirigo*** was in good condition with healthy emigrants on board. The *South Australian Register* on Thursday 23 November 1854 included the following comment:

> *We are gratified to learn that Dr. Duncan, Immigration Agent and Health Officer, is highly pleased with the condition of this ship, the appointments, and everything else conducive to the comfort of the emigrants, who are in excellent health and spirits, and well satisfied with the treatment they have received on board the Dirigo.*

There were 14 deaths (13 infants) and 11 births on the voyage. The vessel was used again, at least on two occasions, to transport emigrants to the colonies. The next passage with government emigrants was in 1859, departing Liverpool on 6 January and arriving in Hobsons Bay on 28 March with 409 emigrants (no record of any deaths). Then again in late 1859 she departed Liverpool on 20 December and arrived in Sydney on 13 April 1860, transporting 448 passengers with one death and three births.

Ship *Dirigo*
(State Library of Victoria)

On balance, is it appropriate for these large North American–built vessels to be branded as death ships? These large vessels with two decks were originally marked as unsafe to transport emigrants with the initial assessment based on the death count. The Emigration Commissioners did acknowledge the North American ships were not at fault. They did comment, had the point of departure been different (as with most other emigrant vessels departing for the Australian colonies), the outcome may have been different. However, in examining the question about whether the reputation was deserved, there were many factors that impact on the assessment. The following were certainly important factors in determining what happened during those passages in 1852–1853:

- The double-deck arrangement was a problem. Lack of ventilation and continual dampness were problems for all steerage passengers, especially those at the second level. There was also a lack of amenities on the second level, particularly water closets. This led to unhygienic practices, particularly at night if a person was ill or disabled because of seasickness.

- Some vessel designers argued North American–built vessels, because of their construction, were far damper and darker than British-built vessels and that the persistent dampness in these ships was unhealthy.

- There were too many emigrants on these vessels on the 1852–1853 voyages to the colonies. This meant: the voyage was extremely unpleasant; privacy was almost impossible; diseases of the nineteenth century (particularly the airborne) could quickly spread; and it was difficult for so many people to be on the main deck at one time and for bedding to be aired easily (which was part of the required routine on emigrant ships) and for all the emigrants to wash their clothes regularly. Using the main deck for exercise, fresh air, washing and airing were all processes laid out by the Emigration Commission as requirements to be supervised by the surgeon superintendent to contribute to a healthy vessel.

- The six vessels that departed in 1852 did so from Liverpool, which was not normally the port of departure for vessels taking emigrants to the Australian colonies. This primarily happened because the available vessels were registered and based in Liverpool. Liverpool in the mid-nineteenth century was an unhealthy place with high levels of sickness and disease. This increased the likelihood that emigrants waiting to board their vessels would come in contact with carriers of these diseases. These diseases included the waterborne cholera; the louse-borne typhus; and the endemic and highly contagious measles, whooping cough and scarlatina. The emigrants were often from rural areas and had not developed any immunity to such diseases. Even though there was a special depot at Birkenhead for emigrants going to Australia, it could only accommodate 400 people at a time. Hence, for these large vessels the emigrants had to be processed in at least two groups. This provided opportunities for those waiting to board to be exposed to the local community and, in some cases, for those that had been processed, but could not embark immediately, to also be exposed.

- The poor state of health of the emigrants chosen for emigration on these vessels meant they had an immune system that was already under strain. For example, many of the highland Scots and rural Irish had been through very difficult times, often living on a subsistence diet over an extended period. Thus, they arrived at the port of embarkation already malnourished.

- The emigrants were not seafaring people and found life at sea difficult. There are many reports and diary entries that show once the vessels left the relative calm of the Mersey River and entered the Irish Sea, many passengers were seasick. For significant numbers this was a reoccurring problem, which was extremely debilitating. There are many stories of parents being so ill they were unable to take care of their children, including mothers being unable to breastfeed infants. Thus, seasickness not only increased the strain on an already stretched immune system but placed children (particularly infants) at risk of malnutrition and care by parents if they became sick.

- The food provided on these voyages was not always appropriate. For example, many of the emigrants were not accustomed to eating meat and so found it hard to digest. There were many Scots onboard these vessels and they were accustomed to eating oatmeal as a dietary staple and found it difficult to cope when it was not available. There are reports some children were unable to eat the food provided and where they did so it often caused diarrhoea, which in some cases led to atrophy and death. The Emigration Commission admitted that the food provided was not suitable for all classes of emigrants. As a result, more appropriate food was provided for future voyages. Also, food was not provided for infants. It was expected the mother would take care of the infant's needs. If the mother was ill from disease or seasickness, this often meant that the infant starved.

- Language was a problem on some voyages because the emigrants spoke only Gaelic or Irish. This meant communicating with the crew, particularly the captain, the surgeon superintendent and the matron was virtually impossible. Therefore, understanding things like the public health requirements, food preparation arrangements, discipline matters and medical advice was extremely difficult. In some other emigration vessels this was recognised as a potential problem and an interpreter was provided, which contributed to a trouble-free passage.

- Many of the emigrants on these vessels were not accustomed to structure and interference in their lives and so adhering to the rules set for the emigrant vessels by the Commission didn't make sense. These rules had been developed and progressively refined from the start of assisted emigration to the colonies to contribute to the welfare and protect the health of emigrants. There was a clear correlation between adherence to the rules and a safe and healthy passage in nineteenth-century emigration vessels.

- The role of the surgeon superintendent was extremely important on nineteenth-century emigration vessels. He was provided with a copy of *Instructions to Surgeons on Emigrant Ships*, which set out his duties, responsibilities and reporting requirements. It was important he enforced the public health requirements on these vessels. This meant ensuring the areas occupied and used by the emigrants were kept clean, they bathed, clothing was washed, bedding was aired and water closets were used properly. On these large vessels an assistant doctor was appointed because of the number of emigrants. However, even with two doctors, the range of public health duties must have been daunting and potentially unmanageable if there were also many sick people to assist. The effectiveness of the doctors in performing their duties would have depended on their skills, experience, determination and application, and on the cooperation and understanding by the emigrants of the importance of what the doctor was attempting to enforce. In the case of these large vessels, some doctors were ineffective, uninterested and derelict, and there were emigrants that did not understand why these rules were necessary because public health practices of the type being enforced were not practiced as part of their previous lifestyle. There are stories of some emigrants failing to accept the advice of the doctor or to follow the doctor's orders.

- The voyage involved a range of climate zones, which meant passengers would endure the oppressive heat of the tropics (possibly for some time if becalmed) and the freezing conditions of the southern latitudes. The tropical heat would have been almost unbearable for steerage passengers, particularly those accommodated on the second level. Passengers would normally spend time on deck during the time in the tropics, but this was difficult on these large vessels because of the number of passengers and the clutter on the decks (a result of inadequate room below to store the passengers' belongings). Passengers were unprepared for the extreme cold and the gigantic seas experienced in the southern latitudes. Many were inadequately dressed for the cold, were often wet because of the large seas and, for some, seasickness returned. For those emigrants who were unwell, these extremes in climate were an added burden and may have decreased their chance of survival.

- Under pressure from the colonies, the Emigration Commissioners relaxed the rules relating to the number of children that could accompany parents. Ordinarily on vessels under the Emigration Commissioner's supervision, families with more than three children under 10, or two under seven, were not permitted to embark. The level of pressure from the colonies and British manufacturers was so intense the commissioners permitted families with four children under the age of 12 to embark. The colonies were interested in families where there were young children, as they felt there was less chance of the father or the whole family moving to the goldfields. With the relaxation of the rules, there were large numbers of young children (including infants) on all these large vessels. They were more susceptible to the airborne diseases, particularly measles. Epidemic diarrhoea often occurred on these voyages, which lowered resistance to childhood infections. The result was that many children (particularly infants) died on these voyages. This type of journey was not suitable or safe for infants; they did not have the stamina and many simply died from malnutrition.

- Prior to embarkation, the surgeon superintendent was responsible for undertaking a final medical 'examination' of each passenger to determine if the passenger was fit to undertake the journey. While it was not possible in the middle of the nineteenth century for doctors to determine if a person had a disease in the incubation phase, it was possible by observation to find tell-tale signs, such as the rash that comes with measles. Many doctors simply asked the person if they were well and the answer was of course yes. Others took time to look carefully at the person and to ask questions that based on their experience, may have assisted in determining if the passenger was fit for the voyage. In the case of these large ships, the surgeon superintendent and his assistant were not given enough time to examine all the bodies, clothing and baggage and hence this process was largely undertaken in a superficial manner. There is evidence that shows where this process was undertaken rigorously with passengers on nineteenth-century emigration vessels, the rate of illness and death was low.

The various reviews, inquiries and investigations show different opinions and conclusions emerged as to the cause of the high death rate on these large North American–built vessels when used on the Australian run. Some of these opinions were coloured by experience (or lack thereof), by people being defensive or sensitive to criticism and, in some cases, being concerned about maintaining their position or receiving their annuity. However, I believe all the factors I have listed above emerge to varying degrees for all the large two-decker vessels used by the Emigration Commission in 1852–1853.

It's interesting to note the conclusion reached by economic historians, John McDonald and Ralph Shlomowitz, from their work investigating mortality of immigrants travelling to the Australian colonies in the nineteenth century. They found there were relationships between the size of the vessel, the length of the voyage and crowding that had a bearing on mortality and the relationship between these variables differed for adults and children. For example, they concluded:

> *The analysis indicates that adult migrant mortality was associated with different characteristics than child and infant mortality. For adults, the main characteristics were length of voyage and the degree of crowding…For children and infants…the length of the voyage and degree of crowding were far more influential. And in addition, the tonnage of the vessel was important. There was a tendency for more infants, and in particular more children to die on bigger ships…for adults, from 1838 to 1853 land-based mortality rates were lower than on immigrant voyages, but after 1853 the rates were similar. In contrast, after 1853 onboard infant and child mortality rates persisted at much higher rates than on land. The very high infant mortality rates on voyages were mainly due to high post neo-natal rates, probably resulting from infectious diseases sweeping through the confined infant population onboard, the difficulty of weaning during a voyage, and increased diarrhoea disease in the tropics. The statistically significant relationship between mortality and variables such as crowding and tonnage in our regression analysis highlight the dangers faced by infants from acute infectious diseases, such as measles, and from diarrhoea disease.*[88]

---

88 McDonald J. & Shlomowitz, R. Mortality on migrant voyages to Australia in the nineteenth century. Flinders University, Working Papers in Economic History, September 1988, No. 25, pp. 17–18.

In the context of looking at deaths on emigrant vessels during the nineteenth century, it's worth remembering over 98 per cent of government-assisted emigrants who departed for the colonies from a United Kingdom port arrived in reasonable health ready to commence a new life. Of those, it seems the two per cent that died at sea, most (possibly around three-quarters) were under the age of six and about half of these were infants aged less than 12 months. Clearly, life at sea in the nineteenth century on long voyages, such as those taken to reach the Australian colonies, was a risky business for children, especially infants. The point of embarkation and the conditions prevailing on the large two-deck vessels created an even higher risk for children than those encountered on single-deck emigration vessels carrying 300–400 passengers.

In terms of transportation for emigrants after 1853, the acting Victorian Immigration Agent made the following comments in his annual report for 1854:

> ...the employment of box vessels of large tonnage, with one passenger deck, both shortens the voyage and diminishes mortality – facts which my predecessors have dwelt upon, and which the Returns for 1854 strongly confirm.
>
> The mortality in ships with Government Emigrants, now that the use of two passenger decks is abandoned, has not reached among the adults the rate of 1.8¾ per cent on the year...
>
> I might point out that this result is signally gratifying, when the space and variety of latitudes to be sailed over are taken into consideration.
>
> I would recommend generally that vessels from 700 to 900 tons, with only one passenger deck be still employed, and that 300 be the maximum of passengers to be carried. When ships of larger tonnage are employed, the additional space is a security for the health

of the passengers, and the ship-owners are not sufferers, inasmuch as their vessels then carry several hundred tons of cargo.[89]

Examples of large vessels with one deck were provided by the immigration agent as proof that large vessels could safely carry emigrants to the colonies. One such large vessel, which also sailed in 1852, was the **Europa** (1088 tons). She carried 492 passengers, taking 90 days for the voyage, and there were only eight deaths. The higher tonnage provided more space for passengers and this type of vessel was faster than the traditional square-rigger. The passenger/tonnage ratio was the key element for safe passage in the future. This was also borne out when the **Shackamaxon**, **Wanata** and **Marco Polo** were used to transport fewer emigrants to the colonies.

In the years leading up to 1852, the Emigration Commission attempted to work co-operatively with the colonies to deliver healthy emigrants in line with the requirements of each colony and at a reasonable economic cost (bearing in mind they were spending colonial money). They had largely managed to achieve this, although the colonies frequently complained the wrong type of emigrants were delivered.[90] As mentioned previously, the Commission had designed and periodically refined sets of rules and regulations for the captain of the vessels, for the surgeon superintendent, for the emigrants and others and had devised a formula to govern the number and ages of children on each vessel. When these procedures and requirements were followed, emigrants were identified, marshalled, inspected, embarked and delivered in most cases without major problems. With these large two-deck vessels, key rules were broken, ignored or modified to suit the circumstances that developed in response to some consequences that followed from the discovery of gold. Government intervention was possibly the most influential factor in achieving a low death rate

---

89 Report of the Acting Immigration Agent, G.W. Rusden for the Year 1854, Melbourne 31 July, 1855. Parliament of Victoria GP V 1855/56 no. A7.

90 See discussion in Limbrick, D. Farewell to Old England Forever. Publicious, 2017, particularly Chapter 4.

on emigration vessels during the nineteenth century. It regulated the selection of emigrants, the type of vessel, the degree of crowding, arrangements on board, and measures for preventing disease. A failure in any of these areas was potentially dangerous to the health of the emigrants.

It is of course possible to reach a conclusion about the undesirability of using the two-decker vessels just by looking at numbers (total number of deaths), but it should be remembered there were also many deaths on some single-deck vessels and the death rate on those single-deck vessels was regarded as high compared to what had become the expected norm by the middle of the nineteenth century. It's also possible to say the death rate on most of the large double-deck vessels was not too different to the average for mid-nineteenth-century emigration vessels for adults and that these vessels were successful in delivering large numbers of people to the colonies at a time when replacement labour was urgently required.

While all these comments may be more or less true, I believe the most significant legacy from using these large double-deck ships was the impact on the people that came in them as emigrants. The enormous discomfort caused by the gross overcrowding that was endured by those beneath the main deck—particularly those on the second deck—would have been extremely difficult to endure, especially when combined with illness, seasickness, the heat of the tropics, and the freezing and wet conditions of the Great Southern Ocean. The diaries of passengers record feelings of alarm and fear of sinking in the enormous seas. The smells below deck from body odour, leaking water closets, seasickness, illnesses (especially typhus) and the whale oil in the lanterns were nauseating. However, the part of the voyage remembered most by many families would have been the death of a family member or members. The grief would have been enormous. They set off looking forward to a new life and new opportunities and arrived without loved ones. The sight and sound of babies wrapped in canvass being tossed overboard would have haunted the families and other passengers for the rest of their lives. I am sure many of them would have regretted the decision they took to emigrate. These were hardy people drawn from many of the depressed areas of Scotland, Ireland and England. They were accustomed to deprivation, poverty and hardship. However, I still think the conditions on these vessels would have left many with terrible memories of the experience.

Each of the six ships were no doubt designed by people with compassion for shipbuilding who aimed to achieve a more efficient, larger and faster vessel. They were then constructed by skilled craftsmen who would have been proud of their work. It seems from shipyard records the designers and builders were proud of what they achieved. The six ships – the ***Bourneuf, Wanata, Marco Polo, Ticonderoga, Beejapore*** and ***Shackamaxon***—were indeed large, fast and wonderful-looking vessels. They received much attention and adoration for their looks. However, they were designed to be able to carry a large amount of cargo and not for carrying large numbers of passengers.

When these vessels were used as single-deck vessels with 400 passengers on one deck, the result was entirely different. The passengers experienced conditions similar to all steerage-class passengers on nineteenth-century emigrant ships, which were generally unpleasant. However, for those on the second deck in the double-deck ships, the conditions were even more deplorable, depressing and difficult to endure. We should not forget they were accommodated in an area only ever intended for cargo. In addition to the physical conditions resulting from location, there was ever present seasickness and disease on an epidemic scale, which must have combined to make it unbearable. While the major loss occurred among the young children and infants there were many adults who, at the end of the voyage, were deeply pained, traumatised and left wondering why on earth they had decided to emigrate. Hopefully time and positive experiences and opportunities in their new home-made coping with the experience possible.

APPENDIX A

GLOSSARY OF TERMS

In order to assist the reader who might be unfamiliar with the nautical terms used in this book, a list of the more common nautical and other unusual nineteenth-century terms are provided in this appendix.

Able-bodied - Refers to an experienced seaman, as distinct from a less experienced ordinary seaman.

Abeam - At or from a point level with the centre of the hull of a vessel.

Amidships - A point midway along the centre-line of a hull, but commonly used for the centre part of a vessel.

Ballast - Heavy substances (including water, if tanks are fitted) carried low down in the hull, to stabilise an empty vessel.

Barquentine - Vessel of three or more masts; square rigged on the fore, fore and aft rigged on the others.

Beam - Width of a hull at its widest point.

Beam ends - A vessel is said to be 'on her beam ends' when forced completely over on her side.

Beam wind - A wind blowing at or close to right angles to the length of the vessel.

Bear up - To turn a vessel's head away from the wind.

Beat - To advance towards the wind by a series of alternate tacks.

Bowspit - Spar projecting from the bows and setting the head-sails.

Brig - Vessel of two masts, square rigged on each.

Broach-to - Describes a vessel unable to be controlled by her helm and lying broadside to high sea, in danger of capsizing or being dismasted.

Catwalk - A railed foot bridge connecting the superstructures on a vessel's main deck.

CLEC - The Colonial Land and Emigration Commission (also referred to as the Emigration Commission).

Clew - Generally refers to the bottom corner of a sail to which sheets are attached to work the sail.

Companion - A stairway leading below from the deck.

Dead-reckoning - Navigation based purely on course and distance, without aid of celestial observation.

Doldrums - Sections of calm, with fickle winds and often heavy rain-squalls, lying between the Trade-wind regions.

Draught - The depth of water required to float a vessel.

Easting - An open area of sea where strong westerly winds prevail (for ships coming to Australia via the Cape of Good Hope these occur below latitude 45 S). These conditions enable fast and continuous eastward sailing. This was referred to as 'running the Easting down'.

Feedin' the fishes - Term used to describe seasick passengers hanging over the side of a vessel.

Forward - Pronounced 'forrard', is towards the bows of a vessel.

Full-rigged - A sailing vessel with three or more masts, all of which are square-rigged.

Galley - Kitchen on a vessel.

Harpie - A person who preyed on travellers waiting to embark ship.

Heave-to - To put a vessel (during bad weather) with her weather bow facing wind and sea, with the sails trimmed, so she rides in that position. May also involve setting her sails aback in order to check forward progress.

Jib - A triangular sail set between foremast and bowsprit.

Ketch - Two-masted, fore and aft rigged vessel, the mizzen being stepped forward on the stern post.

Lee - The side of the vessel away from the wind; opposite to the weather.

Nautical mile - A mile at sea; equal to 1852 metres.

Packet - A passenger vessel engaged in regular mail-carrying service.

Passage - A journey between two ports.

Plain-sail - Full, normal orthodox sail.

Port - The left-hand side of a vessel (facing forward).

Port tack - A vessel sailing with the wind blowing on her port side.

Reefing - To decrease the area of sail by using only the upper section (or reef).

Scuppers - Gully or open drain running around the outer edge of a deck.

Sheets - Ropes, wires or tackles, attached to clews of sails or ends of booms, for working them when sail is set.

Square-rigger - A sailing vessel whose masts carry yards from which square sail is set.

Tack - To put a vessel about by bringing her head across the wind; a series of tacks producing a zigzag course towards the wind.

'Tween decks - Area between decks used to accommodate steerage. passengers.

Veer - To let out a line or cable.

Windlass - A large capstan (drum) employed to raise the anchor.

Windward - The weather side of a vessel; opposite to leeward.

Yards - Spars that cross the masts of a square-rigged vessel. They are attached to the mast at their centre point.

Yard-arm - These are the outer extremities of a vessel's yards.

Bibliography

Bride, T.F. Letters from Victorian Pioneers. Lloyd O'Neil Pty. Ltd., 1983.

Broome, Richard. The Victorians. Arriving. Fairfax, Syme & Weldon Associates, 1984.

Cannon, Michael. Perilous Voyages to the New Land. Today's Australia Publishing Company, 1997.

Crotty, Martin and Roberts, David Andrew eds. Turning Points in Australian History. UNSW Press, 2009.

Cutler, Carl C. Greyhounds of the Sea: the Study of the American Clipper Ship. London, 1930.

Cutler, Carl C. Queens of the Western Ocean: the Story of America's Mail and Passenger Sailing Lines. U.S. Naval Institute, 1961.

Foley, Jean, Duncan. In Quarantine: A History of Sydney's Quarantine Station 1828–1984. Kangaroo Press Pty Ltd, New South Wales, 1995.

Foley, Jean, Duncan. Maritime Quarantine Versus Commerce: The Role of the Health Officer of Port Jackson in the Nineteenth Century. Journal of Royal Australian Historical Society, December 2004, v. 90, no. 2, pp. 152–174.

Gross, Alan. Charles Joseph La Trobe. Melbourne University Press, 1956.

Haines Robin. Doctors at Sea. Emigrant Voyages to Colonial Australia. Palgrave Macmillan, 2005.

Haines, R. and Shlomowitz R. Emigration from Europe to Colonial Destinations, Some Nineteenth Century Australian and South African Perspectives. Flinders University, Working Papers in Economic History, No. 63, August 1995.

Haines, Robin. Life and Death in the Age of Sail. The Passage to Australia. UNSW Press, 2003.

Haines, R. & Shlomowitz, R. Nineteenth Century Immigration from the United Kingdom to Australia, An Estimate of the Percentage Who were Government Assisted. Flinders University, Working Papers in Economic History, No. 45, September 1990.

Hopkins, Eric. Childhood Transformed: Working Class Children in Nineteenth-Century England. Manchester University Press, 1994.

Kruithof, Mary. Fever Beach. QI Publishing Company, 2002.

McDonald, John and Shlomowitz, Ralph. Mortality on Immigrant Voyages to Australia in the Nineteenth Century. Flinders University, Working Papers in Economic History, No. 25, September 1988.

Megalogenis, George. Australia's Second Chance. What our history tells us about our future. Penguin Hamish Hamilton, 2015.

Monaghan, Jay. The Australians and the Gold Rush. University of California Press, 1966.

Mundle, Rob. Under Full Sail. ABC Books, 2016.

Prebble, John. The Highland Clearances. Penguin Books, 1969.

Reeves, Keir. 15 July 1851 Hargreaves Discovers Gold at Ophir: Australia's Golden Age. Chapter 4 in Turning Points in Australian History. Edited by Crotty, Martin and Roberts, David Andrew. UNSW Press, 2009.

Serle, G. The Gold Generation. Victorian Historical Journal, vol. 41, no. 1, 1970.

Stammers, Michael. Emigrant Clippers to Australia. Milepost Research, 1995.

Stammers, Michael. The Passage Makers. Teredo Books, 1978.

Veitch, Michael. Hell Ship: The true story of the plague ship Ticonderoga. Allen & Unwin, 2018.

Woolcock, Helen R. Rights of Passage: Emigration to Australia in the Nineteenth Century. Tavistock Publications, 1986.

Index

Countries, Cities, Places:

Adelaide iii, xv, 6, 8, 9, 14, 114, 149, 152, 157, 158, 160, 161, 163, 164, 166, 167, 169, 170, 172, 184, 187
Africa 37, 175
Atlantic 11, 12, 17, 33, 66, 103, 175
Australia iv, v, xx, xxi, xxii, 1, 2, 3, 5, 10, 12, 13, 14, 16, 17, 18, 35, 42, 43, 47, 48, 54, 55, 56, 57, 58, 60, 63, 66, 68, 70, 71, 74, 89, 93, 96, 101, 104, 109, 129, 131, 161, 163, 169, 177, 183, 184, 186, 189, 194, 200, 203, 204, 205
Australian colonies vii, ix, xix, 1, 2, 3, 6, 11, 12, 13, 19, 33, 34, 35, 47, 48, 67, 84, 86, 159, 160, 162, 174, 181, 188, 189, 194, 195
Ballarat 52, 53
Bay of Biscay 11, 12, 87
Bengal 29, 123
Birkenhead xvi, 47, 48, 70, 95, 109, 110, 120, 129, 159, 170, 174, 186, 189
Bonny (Nigeria) 175
Brisbane 83
Bristol 38
Britain vii, xiii, xv, xxii, xxiii, 2, 13, 19, 20, 23, 24, 27, 28, 30, 33, 34, 35, 38, 47, 56, 66, 67, 84, 97, 132, 150
British Isles 11, 19, 42
California 51, 52, 55, 204
Campbeltown Harbour (Scotland) xvii
Canada v, xv, xxii, 38, 39, 42, 84
Canada Dock 38
Canvas Town 61
Cape Horn 12
Cape Otway 60, 99, 113

Cape Town 3, 12, 13
Circular Quay 174
Clare 69
Clarence Dock 46
Diggings xvi, 53, 54, 58, 59
Doldrums 200
England iii, v, xix, xxi, 1, 2, 7, 11, 19, 27, 28, 31, 37, 39, 46, 56, 57, 65, 84, 97, 108, 128, 129, 132, 144, 155, 163, 167, 196, 198, 204
Europe xxi, 2, 28, 42, 43, 46, 56, 60, 85, 204
Geelong xvi, xxi, 55, 69, 70, 72, 73, 74, 113, 129, 179
Georges Dock 43
Glasgow 81, 99
Goldfields xxi, xxii, 51, 55, 56, 59, 62, 63, 64, 65, 74, 94, 99, 177, 192
Gravesend 149, 150, 163
Great Southern Ocean 15, 98, 102, 104, 112, 197
Greenwich 17
Hobsons Bay 60, 79, 99, 101, 118, 123, 187
Indian Ocean 12, 17
Ireland xix, 37, 46, 82, 84, 85, 86, 89, 149, 150, 183, 184, 185, 198
Keppel Bay 149, 150, 155
Lake George (New York State) 122
Lancashire 28, 38, 39, 150
Leeds 26
Le Havre 43
Liverpool v, xiii, xv, xvi, xxii, xxiii, 25, 34, 35, 37, 38, 39, 40, 41, 42, 43, 44, 45, 46, 47, 65, 66, 69, 77, 79, 81, 82, 86, 87, 90, 92, 94, 95, 97, 98, 99, 100, 101, 103, 104, 105, 108, 109, 114, 117, 126, 127, 130, 131, 148, 149, 158, 160, 161, 162, 163, 166, 169, 170, 171, 172, 174, 175, 178, 182, 187, 189
London xvii, 5, 9, 25, 26, 27, 28, 31, 38, 41, 43, 44, 45, 47, 49, 55, 71, 82, 85, 86, 87, 97, 115, 149, 151, 152, 171, 185, 203
Madeira 12, 149
Manchester 31, 38, 39, 204
Melbourne xvi, xvii, xxi, 52, 53, 55, 57, 58, 59, 62, 64, 79, 80, 81, 82, 87, 93, 94, 95, 97, 98, 99, 101, 102, 103, 104, 105, 113, 114, 115, 118, 119, 120, 121, 133, 163, 170, 171, 173, 179, 196, 203
New Brunswick v, xvi, xvii, 77, 78, 89, 90, 91, 125, 126, 127, 186
New South Wales v, xxii, 51, 52, 55, 60, 68, 101, 104, 127, 128, 131, 132, 136, 137, 139, 140, 142, 145, 146, 170, 174, 177, 203
New World 42, 46, 175
New York 107, 108, 122, 123
New Zealand 13, 14, 34, 42, 43, 60, 84, 99

North America xxii, 30, 33, 34, 38, 42, 43, 44, 65, 66, 67, 121
North Atlantic 11, 12
Nova Scotia 69
Peru 146, 155
Philadelphia 157, 158, 161
Plymouth xv, 7, 12, 14, 43, 47, 37
Point Gellibrand 60
Port Jackson xvii, 127, 131, 132, 133, 134, 145, 146, 147, 203
Portland 8, 151, 179
Port Phillip xvii, 52, 60, 61, 97, 99, 103, 105, 113, 116, 117, 118, 123, 130, 133, 173
Prince Edward Island 106
Queenstown (Ireland) 82, 85, 86, 149, 151, 152, 153, 184, 185
Queen's Wharf 118, 119
Rio de Janeiro 12
River Mersey 38, 39
River Yarra 61
River Yarra Yarra (also Yarra River) 99, 118
Saint John River 89
Scotland xvii, xix, 28, 38, 46, 94, 122, 180, 183, 184, 185, 198
Southampton 43, 47, 82, 148
South Atlantic 11, 12
South Australia v, xxii, 2, 13, 14, 16, 60, 68, 101, 161, 169, 177, 183, 184
Southern Ocean 3, 9, 15, 98, 102, 104, 112, 197
Summer Hill Creek 51
Sunderland 28
Sydney 11, 52, 86, 123, 130, 131, 133, 135, 136, 137, 138, 140, 142, 145, 146, 148, 150, 154, 155, 171, 174, 187, 203
Sydney Heads 131
Tasmania 60, 85
Torres Strait 74
United Kingdom xix, xx, xxi, 1, 2, 57, 58, 60, 185, 195, 204
United States xxi, xxii, 29, 161, 166
Valparaiso 105
Victoria iii, v, xxi, xxii, 8, 10, 15, 16, 20, 26, 47, 52, 53, 54, 55, 56, 58, 59, 60, 61, 62, 64, 65, 66, 68, 69, 72, 80, 82, 96, 100, 101, 105, 106, 109, 110, 113, 115, 116, 117, 118, 120, 122, 128, 145, 170, 171, 173, 177, 178, 180, 183, 184, 185, 187, 195
Wales v, xxii, 31, 37, 51, 52, 55, 60, 68, 101, 104, 127, 128, 131, 132, 136, 137, 139, 140, 142, 145, 146, 170, 174, 177, 203
Waterloo Docks xvi, 47

West Indies 37, 42
Williamsburgh 107
Williamstown xvii, 79, 103, 114, 118
Yorkshire xxi, 62

Diseases/Illnesses:

Catarrh 98
Cholera 28, 41
Croup 31, 32
Diarrhoea 25, 29, 70, 71, 98, 111, 114, 190, 193, 194
Diphtheria 32, 34, 35
Influenza 24, 27
Measles 31, 32, 34, 35, 70, 71, 80, 98, 99, 131, 134, 139, 145, 154, 180, 189, 193, 194
Pneumonia 98
Scarlatina 70, 112, 114, 121, 159, 160, 162, 165, 189
Scarlet fever 32, 34, 35, 70, 132, 134, 145, 153, 169, 180
Seasickness 5, 8, 9, 10, 14, 95, 98, 110, 111, 151, 188, 190, 192, 197, 198
Smallpox 31, 32, 34, 42, 132, 133, 134, 183, 184
Tuberculosis 23, 27, 28, 34
Typhoid and Typhoid Fever 25, 27, 29, 30, 34, 81, 145
Typhus 5, 24, 27, 29, 30, 33, 41, 79, 80, 111, 112, 113, 114, 117, 118, 132, 134, 145, 180, 184, 189, 197
Whooping Cough 31, 35, 79, 98, 189

Newspapers/Publications:

Adelaide Times 164, 166
Argus 53, 54, 56, 70, 73, 103, 114, 119, 120, 172, 173
Australian and New Zealand Gazette 99
Bathurst Free Press 51
Buchan's Domestic Medicine 32
Cornwall Chronicle 103
Courier 83, 85, 91, 149, 170, 171
Empire 114, 116, 117, 174
Geelong Advertiser and Intelligencer 129
Illustrated Australian News 10, 61
Illustrated London News xvii, 5, 47, 49, 71, 97, 185
Irish Medical Times 29
London Medical Gazette 27
London Times 44, 45, 55

New Brunswick Courier 91
New South Wales Government Gazette 136
Rockhampton Bulletin and Central Queensland Advertiser 154
Salisbury and Winchester Journal 108
South Australian Register 7, 13, 162, 168, 178, 187
Sydney Morning Herald 86, 131, 138, 146
The Adelaide Observer 157

Occupations:

Gold miner 52, 55
Medical Officer of Health (MOH) 40

Organisations:

Black Ball Line 82, 89, 93, 94, 95, 96, 104, 105, 149
Black Star Line 108
British Government 6, 161
Colonial Land & Emigration Commission (also Emigration Commission or Commission). 63
House of Commons 62, 63, 181
Immigration Board of Geelong 72
Merseyside Maritime Museum 39, 43, 175
Queensland Government 84, 85, 149, 150
Queensland Immigration Society 83, 85, 150
White Star Line 44

People/Positions:

Abijou Good 151
Aboriginal Australians 35
Alan Gross 62
Bishop Quinn 152
Captain Bull 106
Captain Charles Ferguson 105, 114
Captain Drenning 148, 149, 152
Captain J. Lee 79
Captain Robert Biddy 69
Captain West 158, 165, 166, 167
Capt. Arnold xvii, 104
Capt H.H. Brown 142
Charles Dickens 64
Dr. Barnetts 141

Dr Belinfante 149
Dr. Duncan 160, 161, 163, 187
Dr Haynes Alleyne 133, 134, 136, 138, 141, 142, 143, 144
Dr Hunt 79, 115, 117
Dr. Sanger 110, 113, 117
Dr Trench 40, 41
Duke of Newcastle 181, 183
Earl Grey 55
E. Deas Thomson 128
Edward Grimes 81, 178
Edward Hargraves 51
Edward Jenner 24
Edwin Bird 102
Forbes 96, 97, 98, 99, 101, 102, 103, 104
Francis Taylor 6, 8
Frederick Wallace 92
Geoffrey Serle 57
George Stafford xv, xvi, 20, 53
Governor xxi, 51, 52, 55, 128, 136, 165, 169, 183
Governor FitzRoy 51, 55
Governor La Trobe xxi
Henry Wadsworth Longfellow 107
Herman Merivale 181
Immigration Agent 163, 165, 178, 187, 195, 196
Irish 29, 30, 33, 40, 41, 43, 45, 46, 48, 69, 73, 85, 95, 108, 109, 110, 151, 153, 182, 189, 190
Jacob Steere-Williams 30
James Baines 92
James Fawsett 164, 166
James Nicol Forbes (also James Forbes or 'Bully' Forbes) or Captain Forbes) 96
James Smith xvi, 89, 90, 91, 92
Major Duncan Campbell 122
Martin Hollenberg 91
Paddy McGee 92
Parsons 2
Port Health Officer 80, 115, 117
Rev Curley 86
Rev. John Wilson 86
Robert Dudley xv, 38, 39
Robert Louis Stevenson 23
Scots 69, 70, 109, 122, 150, 189, 190

Scottish highlanders 33, 98
Secretary of State (for the colonies) 41, 62, 66, 180, 181
Sir Henry Edward Fox Young (also Governor Fox Young) 163
S.T. Gill xvi, xvii, 61, 120
Surgeon Superintendent 6, 7, 10, 11, 68, 73, 74, 79, 82, 83, 94, 110, 117, 127, 134, 136, 140, 141, 142, 149, 158, 159, 163, 164, 172, 174, 189, 190, 191, 193, 196
Thomas Boyle (also Capt Boyle) 110, 116
T. R. Miles 138
Ursula Henriques 24
Victorian Colonial Secretary 65, 178
Victorian health officer 71
Victor Turner 56
William Campbell 52, 157
William Culshaw Greenhalgh 102
William Penn 157, 158
William Thompson 8
William Thomson 79
William Veitch 110, 117, 205
W. Usherwood 140

Periods:

Middle Ages 29
Nineteenth century xix, xx, xxii, 1, 2, 3, 4, 11, 19, 20, 23, 24, 29, 31, 32, 33, 34, 35, 41, 42, 47, 68, 89, 99, 111, 131, 172, 185, 188, 189, 193, 194, 195, 197
Victorian Britain xiii, xv, xxii, xxiii, 23, 30

Products:

Gold xiii, xvi, xx, xxi, xxiii, 2, 4, 11, 12, 13, 43, 48, 51, 52, 53, 54, 55, 56, 57, 59, 60, 62, 63, 64, 65, 72, 82, 89, 93, 99, 119, 128, 146, 157, 166, 167, 178, 179, 196, 204
Wheat xxi, 56
Wool xxi, 37, 55, 56, 62, 166, 167

Ships:

Apollo 79
Beejapore xiii, xvii, 67, 125, 127, 128, 129, 130, 131, 135, 136, 137, 138, 139, 140, 142, 143, 145, 146, 148, 149, 150, 151, 152, 153, 154, 155, 198
Bourneuf xiii, xvi, 67, 69, 70, 71, 72, 73, 74, 79, 94, 179, 180, 181, 182, 198
Brightman 7
Britannia 44

Bussorah Merchant 132
City of Mobile 149, 152
Cleopatra 96
Condor xvii, 130
Constance xv, 13, 14
Director 134
Dirigo xvii, 186, 187
Donald Mackay 84
Eagle 57
Empire 114, 116, 117, 174
Europa 196
Eutopia 155
Everton 42, 82
Fanny 80
Harmony 143
HMS Hercules (Hercules) xvii, 183, 184, 185
Kent 16
Lady MacNaghten 132
Loch Broom xv, 15
Lysander 114, 116, 117, 118
Maitland 69, 118
Marco Polo xiii, xvi, xvii, 67, 89, 90, 91, 92, 93, 94, 95, 96, 97, 98, 99, 100, 101, 102, 103, 104, 105, 106, 125, 179, 180, 181, 182, 186, 196, 198
Maria 96
Marmion 8, 9
Mobile 117, 149, 152
Morning Light 113
Ottillia 114, 117
Queen of Beauty 87
Ranger 113
Red Jacket xv, 16
Revolving Light xvii, 126
Shackamaxon xiii, xvii, 67, 157, 158, 159, 160, 161, 162, 163, 164, 166, 167, 168, 169, 170, 171, 172, 173, 174, 175, 178, 186, 187, 196, 198
Sir John Lawrence 152
Stag iii, xv, 6, 8, 18
Surrey 25, 132
Ticonderoga xiii, xvii, 67, 107, 108, 109, 110, 112, 113, 114, 115, 116, 117, 118, 119, 120, 121, 122, 123, 179, 180, 181, 198, 205
Titanic 44
Wanata xiii, xvi, 67, 77, 79, 80, 81, 82, 83, 85, 86, 87, 94, 150, 179, 180, 181,

182, 186, 196, 198
White Star 44, 126

Words:

Assisted Passage xix, 44, 56, 72
Barque xv, 4
Clipper ships 90, 107
Emigration xix, xx, xxiii, 2, 7, 8, 19, 23, 33, 34, 35, 43, 45, 46, 48, 56, 62, 63, 66, 68, 71, 74, 75, 84, 85, 95, 128, 148, 149, 150, 160, 164, 169, 172, 177, 181, 182, 183, 189, 190, 191, 193, 195, 197
Endemic xxii, 24, 27, 29, 30, 31, 33, 34, 35, 94, 189
Epidemic xxii, 24, 27, 29, 33, 41, 42, 98, 111, 112, 155, 198
Gaelic 73, 120, 121, 190
Great Circle Sailing 13
Great Irish Famine 33
Highland Clearances 33, 204
Immigration 63, 85, 134, 164, 171, 179, 180, 196
Latitude 17
Longitude 17, 85, 101, 149
Mutiny 82
Passenger Vessels Act 33
Quarantine 33, 70, 71, 79, 80, 81, 82, 113, 116, 117, 118, 120, 122, 123, 131, 132, 133, 134, 135, 136, 140, 143, 145, 146, 147, 149, 161, 174, 178, 180, 184, 185
Quarantine Act 132, 133
Roaring Forties 11
Slaves 37
Slave trade 42, 175
Square rigged 3, 91, 199, 200
Square-rigger 9, 196
Steamship 43
Steerage xv, xx, 4, 5, 6, 8, 21, 34, 66, 79, 84, 93, 94, 95, 96, 110, 129, 150, 167, 175, 188, 192, 198, 202
Trade Winds 11, 12

Shawline Publishing Group Pty Ltd
www.shawlinepublishing.com.au

www.ingramcontent.com/pod-product-compliance
Lightning Source LLC
Chambersburg PA
CBHW040415100526
44588CB00022B/2828